CHANGING THE WORLD
from the inside out

CONNECTING YOUR INTELLIGENCES

Michael Meegan

Changing the World

from the inside out

Connecting your Intelligences

Michael Meegan

DEDICATION

This book is dedicated to a man who heals, to a man who has spent much of his life caring for others. For decades he has quietly reached out to the poor, making a difference in the lives of those he met. As a surgeon he has performed hundreds of operations in primitive conditions. As a physician he treats everyone who comes to him with gentleness and respect. He always has time, always says "yes". As a teacher he has trained many obstetricians and gynaecologists, sharing his infectious passion for serving others. As a father Evan has nurtured creative, caring children full of love and their fathers empathy. As a man, Evan embraces life with delight and selflessness enriching those he meets. And as a friend... the greatest blessing anyone could imagine. Evan continues to change the world around him with joy and delight, humility and passion.

Evan, this is for you!

Dr. Evan Sequeira is a senior obstetrician and gynaecologist. He is a member of the faculty of the Department of Obstetrics and Gynaecology at the Aga Khan University Hospital, Nairobi. He is an internationally respected expert in reproductive health, lecturing around the world and is a research consultant for the World Health Organisation. Evan is head of the ICROSS surgical team and chairman of ICROSS in Kenya.

Changing the World from the Inside Out, First Edition

Published by Eye Books Ltd 2007
8 Peacock Yard
Iliffe Street
London
SE17 3LH

Tel. +44 (0) 845 450 8870
www.eye-books.com

Typeset in Garamond

ISBN-10: 1 9030704 49
ISBN-13: 9781903070444

Printed and bound in Great Britain by CPI Bookmarque, Croydon

Contents

INTRODUCTION

This simple and priceless gift, the secret of joy, is the same as the secret of staying in love. It is about becoming love itself

We live in a world which changes before our eyes - the economy, the climate, demands and intrusions in the name of security — all change almost daily, and all impact on the way we live. Computers, digital television, mobiles and new generations of IT pour into our lives at an ever-accelerating broadband pace. We have never known so much, had so much, nor travelled so much. We have more computer power in our mobile phones than there was on the Apollo craft that took three men to the moon and back in the 1960s. While our lives are tossed on tides of transformation, it is worth taking stock of our role, in the midst of all this change.

The economy, the climate, the demands and intrusions in the name of security; all impact on the way we live

Modern society actually depends upon us being stressed and unsatisfied – the anxiety that generates unhappiness and division is the very mechanism that makes us want to buy things that we don't need. There is a frenetic hurry and urgency to everyday life; it feeds off the mythology of progress. It offers money, power, status and stuff, but at the price of our selves. If we ever want to live to our full potential, we need to connect with our dreams, and the power within us, to free ourselves. Anxiety, negative thinking and stress-inducing mind games are habits. We can transform our habits to generate positive thinking and action; it is only a choice, a freedom, handing ourselves power. Habits determine the amount and quality of time we give to our actions.

Most of my time is spent among the desert nomads in East Africa. On the surface it would appear that these pastoral tribes are in total harmony with nature and each other. The romantic version of their lives is that these warriors, the Maasai, have remained unchanged for centuries but that their way of life is now threatened by the coming of the Western World into their peaceful balance with nature. The reality is better than fiction. Darwin never suggested survival of the fittest but put forward that evolution was about adaptation. The Maasai migrated across the Rift Valley in the early sixteenth century and pushed weaker tribes before them as they moved great herds of cattle southwards. The plains that have traditionally been the homelands of the Maasai have had

Do you have your life?
Of course not.
Life has you

repeated droughts, and as the cycles of water short-ages occur every four or five years, deserts spread and climates change. The Maasai are faced with a diffi-cult transition. No longer truly nomadic, they have to explore new types of farming, other sources of livelihood, new ways to live and irrigate. They con-stantly have to learn, adapt and innovate. This becoming, this adaptation is the secret of progress, which creates positive constructive futures.

We too can progress and evolve, by accepting our-selves as we are, and the world as it is: beautiful, magical and perfectly flawed. From this position, we can start to change, to evolve ourselves into who we want to be.

Many years ago, something came into my life that I

had neither expected nor ever could have imagined. It was something that changed my life forever, everything that I was. It altered the way I thought, it changed the way I would live my life and the way I would wake up in the morning. Like everything that is essential, it came free into my life. The things that matter, the gift of life itself, the ones we love, these are all un-beckoned, they are because they are. So too is this very simple and priceless gift, the secret of joy. It is the same as the secret of staying in love. It is about becoming love itself.

This book is about the secret of joy. It is about discovering wonder; becoming our whole selves.

I want to share what I have learned in the hope that it touches within you the something that burns within us all. I offer it to you in the frailty of my own humanity with trembling hands. Whatever there is within these thoughts, take into yourself and let the rest pass from you. We are surrounded by distractions and noise, and our lives are pulled about by countless demands for attention. When I read something, I want it to bring beauty into my life, enrich my heart, touch my mind, help me to see more clearly. My hope is that these words will awaken the wonderful in you and remind you of the power within.

There is a way to transform the whole world. There is a path by which you can become pure beauty. It is not a path of self-help or self-preoccupation. It is a path of discovering the primal spark, of finding the boundless power and light that lie inside you, and being healed by it. It is in fact the opposite of self-help; it is the realisation that joy is not derived through self-absorption but by emptying yourself so that you can be filled with grace.

Becoming the person you always dreamed of rests on three principles:

> *1 We are in search of happiness, and we are open to finding it.*
>
> *2 We need love above all else. Within us is the deep longing to be loved and the desire to give love.*
>
> *3 We often lack the happiness we dream of, and the acceptance and love we need to be whole.*

While life can really affect us, it is how we choose to respond that will shape our attitude, our behaviour, our emotions and our future. I once stayed in a slum in Rio, with a woman and her six children. They lived in a hut made from plastic and cardboard boxes. It was tiny and clean and everyone slept on the ground. Feza was a street cleaner, and the children were fed and went to school. It transpired that three of the children were hers; the others were children who had nowhere else to go. She is one of those Mamas who hugs every child she sees, she had never heard the word 'cannot,' and had no time for sorrow. When I asked her why she took in the other children, she couldn't grasp the question. She looked at me and said, 'Why, wouldn't you bring them in?' Regardless of her own poverty, the only option for Feza, being Feza, was to welcome everyone who came her way and at least one person who didn't - Fabricio tried to steal her rice in the market and she ended up bringing him home. Feza changes the world. And if she can, we all can.

My good friend Ronán said, 'People behave as though you could get happiness inside you by consuming it in some way. This is very similar to another mistake that Europeans make, which is that they think of life as being inside them, "theirs" in some way. The Maasai could put them right on that. People say "he lost his life," or "you ruined my life," or "I dedicated my life to," my life, my life, my life. But let's get this straight; did you have your life? No, of course not. Life had

In all time, in all creation, there will only ever be one of you

you. You were life's decision, not the other way around.'

Only when we see the fullness of humanity, where we are in the here and now, in all its darkness and contradictions, can we look honestly at what really matters. This reflection is an invitation to feel the fire in your heart's centre, and the full flowering of your spirit as it creates light and wonder in the fabric of the here and now. Through this book, we will examine some of the parts of our selves, the components of our intelligence, and some strategies for supporting and empowering them.

A friend's daughter is going through a terrible patch. Aged eight, she is desperate for her parents to be normal. She doesn't want a mother who wears no makeup, who cooks all the food that the family eats, who is totally un-materialistic. She wants a made-up mum, she wants her school friends to be given the same junk food they eat at home when they come to call, she wants her house to be full of the same clutter that fills everyone else's. She is desperate. 'I want to die,' she told her mother, 'I want to stop breathing!'

Try it, I thought. Try to stop breathing, then see who is boss. The life inside you won't let you stop breathing. It's not your life, you cannot own it, so don't think of it that way. As long as you think of yourself as owning your life, you are inside out. When you look outside and see the life that has you, then you will start to be happy.

There will only ever be one of you in all time, in all creation. You are wonder; you are the only one of you who will ever live the miracle and power that is within you.

STARTING WHERE WE ARE

Change always begins at the same place, and at the same time. It begins here and now

I ntelligence and wisdom are gifts that we all have, and we all have them in different proportions. We can get to know them, and learn to nurture them. Intelligence is experience understood and integrated, and wisdom is intelligence of the heart. Our journey starts by knowing where we are, and finding where we want to go. It involves unlearning what we know, seeing things in new ways and engaging dynamically in how we perceive. To live all our lives to the full, celebrating the love within us, we need to understand ourselves, respect ourselves and cherish who we are. Doing this with gentleness will protect us in times of pain. This is the path of self-awareness, the way of wisdom. It is doing something rare, cultivating our many levels of intelligence and perception. How we think about things and the way we understand is deeply rooted in early learning.

This section of the book has tools that we can use to make changes within ourselves. Our changes will be simple and are easily begun, yet they are so fundamental as to begin changing the world around us. We will look at the intelligence that we all have, and see it in its component parts. That way, we can begin to nourish and care for them in turn. We will also look at ways in which the very powerful techniques of meditation, neuro-linguistic programming, mind-mapping and time management can be used together, to put us on a path of change. The examples here are very easy to learn and perform, and they can have a huge effect.

Intelligence is experience understood and integrated, wisdom is intelligence of the heart.

When we look past the distractions of daily 'stuff' and think beyond the traps that tie us to habits, we begin to see a new world around us. This is the nature of deeper knowledge, the nature of wisdom. It awakens the power of wonder and opens the gates of grace. It is about becoming the you within. All wisdom and light is about finding joy and being really happy. At its core, it is about living your dreams, being fully human, fully alive. In the end it is about the reason to live and the reason to die. This is all about the secret of love. So that is what this book is about, the only thing that really matters when everything else has been forgotten, the only thing that is everlasting; love.

Knowledge is a store of information, intellect is the ability to use that knowledge. Intelligence is the gift of seeing relationships between unconnected facts, people, places and things. Seeing and creating patterns. Wisdom is seeing beyond the visible and the distractions of life into reality. To be wise is to grasp the reality beyond the illusions. Wisdom is the light that creates harmony in chaos, and sees into the pure heart of things. Wisdom is knowing how to place life and energy into the things that bring this love into our lives.

Intelligences

> *What a piece of work is man*
> *How noble in reason*
> *how infinite in faculties*
> *in form and moving*
> *how express and admirable*
> *in action how like an angel*
> *in apprehension, how like a god*
> *the beauty of the world*
> *the paragon of animals!*

Shakespeare

In 1983, Howard Gardner identified in *Frames of Mind: The Theory of Multiple Intelligences,* seven intelligences: logical-mathematical, verbal-linguistic, spatial-mechanical, musical, bodily, social-interpersonal, and Self-intrapersonal intelligence. Since then, Daniel Goleman wrote about emotional intelligence, which is part social intelligence and part self intelligence. To these I would add creative intelligence and spiritual intelligence.

How we understand and use these intelligences

affects everything we are, and everything that we do. Becoming aware of the parts that each of these gifts play in our thinking, we become better able to make use of them.

Before you read any further, take a moment to consider these questions:

If you ever had any free time, which of these would you enjoy;

Solving SuDoku, or other number puzzles?
Tinkering with websites or computer programs?

Practicing or learning languages?
Solving crossword puzzles?

Visualising or studying geometric patterns?
Interior or garden design?

Playing or singing harmony with a group or orchestra?
Discovering new pieces of music?

Ball games like softball, tennis or football?
Choreographed or chorus line dancing?

Hosting parties or dinner parties?
Organising picnics or excursions?

Reading or retreats for self-discovery?
Travelling by yourself?

> *Making your fantasies into stories, art or music?*
> *Theatre or costume design?*
>
> *Meditation?*
> *Learning about other people's faiths or cultural*
> *traditions?*

Write your answers down, and keep them in mind, as you read on.

Logical-mathematical intelligence involves our daily logical calculations, reasoning, planning, use of rational and analytical thinking. How often today have you deduced or induced, added or weighed a situation, measured the time to reach home or to collect a friend? Often misunderstood as numerical ability, this is much more about the ability to identify and manipulate abstract patterns and to solve problems using reasoning and logic.

Commanding words can be about knowing when not to use them. Sometimes the most eloquent response is to say nothing.

I remember an exhibition of stunt driving. Cars span at full speed, manoeuvred with balletic precision, flipped over ramps, span in the air and landed perfectly. As with all things well done, it looked effortless. One of the drivers explained how the stunts were accomplished with meticulous and split second accuracy. It required his being completely aware of what was happening outside, the wind, the ground, the space, and success depended on total concentration. If we apply that to ourselves, many of our own judgments and calculations could be enriched. Problem solving is something that we all do every day, we calculate, assess, measure. Whether crossing the road safely or kicking a ball we are making many calculations at the same time.

Verbal-linguistic intelligence is how we command language, articulate our emotions, communicate our thoughts, express ourselves and share what is within us. It is our power to grasp and interpret the nuances of language. Verbal intelligence gives us mastery of the meaning within words, and is quick to spot the unspoken messages behind them. It enables us to connect with others through speech and the written word.

A friend studying French literature at university was bright, funny and gifted with words. He and his girl-friend were having arguments, which often become bitter and angry. There would be a trigger, often an incidental observation, or a comment. An emotional response followed, and my friend would then try to reason. His command of language, his logic and his rationale only seemed to widen the divide, his girl-friend becoming more distant and upset. He began to realise that she was feeling intimidated by his articulation. She knew she would never win an argument and the only way she could respond was with her emotions. My friend began responding to frustration and pain by simply hugging his girlfriend. He learnt something that university could not teach him, that commanding words is often about knowing when not to use them. Sometimes the most eloquent response is to say nothing.

Spatial-mechanical intelligence is the awareness and sense of physical and dimensional space. It is the ability that enables us to judge distances and volumes. This intelligence provides a keen sense of direction, an ease with reading maps and finding the way through unfamiliar places, and comes with a strong visual memory. Visual intelligence helps us to find our way around the physical world, and to imagine physical improvements that we can make to it.

People forget what you say, but will always remember your breath, the you within your sound.

Sculpture has long been a hobby of mine. Creating sculpture, making something three dimensional, is challenging. A teacher gave me a very helpful insight. 'A lot of people look with their eyes when they try to understand form. Close your eyes and touch. What you feel sometimes tells you more about form than what you see, it helps you to understand the depth and shape.' It worked. Somehow trusting my fingers allowed a different experience, one where I could make the forms more alive, more real. Closing our eyes can free us to open our spatial awareness.

Musical intelligence is what makes us distinguish and respond to pitch, timbre, rhythm and tone. This gift is possessed by us all in some degree, and there are Sufi masters who say that the soul's first attachment is to music. Life is made up of pulses and vibrations, and we all have an instinctive affinity with harmonious and energising sounds. Training and nurturing this gift connects us with the audible world, hearing the subtleties of accents and tones of voice, and spotting individual voices in crowds.

Learning African tribal languages, I struggled with the tonal sounds. The pitch and inflection of a single tone can change the meanings. Lemoite Lemako, a young warrior who was teaching me, had a voice like music. He always spoke softly, deliberately. He taught me something the underlying harmony of speech that changed the way I heard and used language. He said, 'people forget what you say, but will always remember your breath, the you within your sound. We can be known from how we speak. Our peace or stress is in our words, and we cant hide from it. It is just us. People hear your harmony, and your words are only a voice of this peace. your words should be on your breath not in your mouth. Soft, not heavy.' The breath that carries your sound holds the rhythm of conversation, giving it music and resonance.

Bodily intelligence embraces our physical selves and our being. A respect, a caring for and a knowledge of ourselves, it includes how we sleep, sit, eat, walk and the way that we breathe. Every gesture, every movement, is a syllable in the body languages that we learn, adopt and make our own. The way that we hold our bodies while we are reading this book and how we look in the mirror are part of our unspoken communication with the world. It is our physical expression, and a celebration of who and what we are.

If you watch a small child learning to crawl, learning to walk, to bounce, to hold things in their chubby little hands, you see how it all works, how much we learn physically, and how we learn from direct experience. For every little step that a toddler takes, there have been countless rear end landings. Babies are great examples of discovering our bodies because its all such an overwhelming delight and full time job. As with all physical learning it is all down to hard work.

Learning to accept and value ourselves as we are is deeply linked to our sense of well-being.

Social-interpersonal intelligence is about how we are with each other, our balance, presence, energy and sharing with those we meet. It is how we interact with others; what we put out, and how we read what we get back. Developing our ability to connect and to accept, enables us to be comfortable with people, and to make them comfortable with us. We have all met people who make us feel fantastic. There are people who are magnetic, with whom you can just open up completely; and we can learn from their example.

When we visit another's home, we feel the energy that fills the space, taste the welcome, and smell the atmosphere. We can be in a mansion and feel unwelcome or in a hovel and feel utterly embraced. Much of this energy is to do with the behaviour, perception, character and love of the people you are with, and this is expressed all the time in the way we live, the way we treat each other and the presence we generate. Our embrace, our hug, our kiss, our warmth, these are part of us and were often cultivated unconsciously by the love that surrounded us as we grew up; such graces form the fuel of life and act as a beacon to others.

Self-intrapersonal intelligence is self knowledge, and without it the other intelligences remain in hibernation. This is the most amazing earth-shaking journey of all, discovering all the wonder and power inside us, freeing us to be who we can be. Those who are innately happy and calm, have a good self intelligence. They realise within themselves the attitude, disposition and state that maximises experience. Learning to accept and value ourselves as we are, is deeply linked to our personal happiness, and the sense of well-being that we feel.

Stella had three locks on her door, because she had still been robbed twice in the past year. The robberies left her changed. She did not sleep as well and she worried. Her neighbours, like her, were elderly, and most lived alone, most were afraid. One afternoon, a group of friends decided that were tired of living in fear, weary of always being scared. This little meeting decided that they would organize themselves. They began to network, started sharing ideas and began an awareness group. They visited each other in the months that followed, and their numbers grew from five to ten, then ten became twenty. Single mothers joined, a young man in a wheelchair, and so did an Asian family who had grills on their windows. Stella found new friends, new purpose and new strength. She slept better after a busy day organizing, and one day she noticed that she no longer saw a frightened old woman in the window. The haggard, worried expression, was gone. Her door still had three locks, but behind it wasn't quite the same old lady. Stella had discovered a new sense of herself.

> *We cultivate the habits of creativity when we look at things from a different angle.*

Creative intelligence is the ability to see solutions outside the constraints of the problem. It is the ability to imagine something that does not exist, and bring it into being. It can be expressed in painting, cooking, gardening or designing. Creative intelligence is the spirit that crafts an idea or a fantasy, to make it into a reality. We would surely teach children better if we encouraged them to think creatively, instead of cramming them with facts and test-passing skills. The more innovation, flexibility and openness we can bring with our approach to life, the more opportunities we can create. Creativity is not only in sculpture and art, it is fresh approaches and perspectives brought to any situation. The more we do this, the more we see the fantastic range of opportunities before us.

In 1993, an Englishman, Trevor Baylis, watched a documentary about AIDS in Africa. Radio was the most effective medium for health education, but the cost of batteries made it too expensive to be widely accessible. His response was to produce a clockwork, wind-up radio. Creative insights often come when we least expect them, but we cultivate the habits of creativity when we look at things from a different angle, or in a different language.

Spiritual intelligence tastes the infinite, knows the light that is within us all. It is the sense of being connected, a part of something far greater. Spiritual intelligence is the sense of the whole of our intelligences making something greater than their sum. It sees the same goal in the quest of the Buddhist, the Muslim, the Pagan and the Christian, as well as the Shaman and the Shaolin monk, to name just a few. Whichever of the follow parallel paths we take, spiritual intelligence is what guides us towards the greater understanding.

Sara came from the slums, she had been abused as a child, and sold into the sex trade. She was brought from Eastern Europe to work backstreet brothels of Amsterdam. Drugs had helped for a while, 'but things only got worse, there was no knight in shining amour.' Too tired to be angry one very dark night, she took herself and a bottle of whisky to the railway track. On a quiet section of track she lay down, looking straight up, her neck on a rail. 'I started to see things, lots of things, there were stars. Thousands of stars. I don't think I ever actually looked at stars like that before, I never actually looked up and ever saw them with my own eyes, only in films. They were beautiful, so different to my sick lost life. They were so beautiful, so clear, so pure.' This could so easily have been the end of Sara's life, but instead, from that insight, it became a new beginning. 'It dawned on me, as I stared into the sky how totally infinite and perfect it was, how unending, how fantastic. An In some way, in maybe a very little way I am a part of all that, I had a strange idea, that I was somehow a very tiny part of something really great. That's when I decided not to kill myself. Something was looking after me that night because there were no trains for an hour.'

Only you know where your strengths and challenges lie.

Sara is now a counsellor for a women's refuge in Amsterdam and part of a growing support group.

Spiritual intelligence is becoming fully human, fully alive, it is about being awake, becoming in touch with everything that we are within. It is the difference between talking about life and living it, it's not about religion but how we are, every action, though, word, the energy we give and receive. Spiritual awareness is wisdom, being free of the traps of others and the limitations of creeds.

FEEDING OUR INTELLIGENCES

Regularly thinking back over the previous day, and identifying how we have used our intelligent energies, helps us to nurture them. If you think back over your last twenty-four hours, you will be able to spot some examples of your intelligences, and of how you used them. Becoming mindful of your gifts will help you to make the best of them. Only you know where your strengths and challenges lie, where the voids and the powerhouses of reserves are. Sometimes these energies are so dominant that they define us or are seen as central in our personality.

The answers that you gave to the questions on pages 23 and 24 will give clues as to how you think of yourself in relation to these intelligences. The first pair of questions was about logical-mathematical intelligence, the second about verbal - linguistic intelligence, and so on in order. Do you think that your answers give an accurate reflection of your innate abilities? Do you see areas where practice may help you make better use of some intelligences?

Putting more energy into the areas in which we are naturally gifted can set up virtuous circles; the results give us joy, and this in turn encourages us to do more, and do better.

Tools and techniques

*We are such stuff as dreams are made on, rounded
with a little sleep*

Meditation, neuro-linguistic programming (NLP) and mind-mapping offer powerful techniques which can help us to connect our intelligences, better understand and know ourselves and those around us, and bring mindfulness to our actions. Some time management can help us to plan and organise our growth, and keep us on track.

This section contains brief descriptions of those disciplines, and I have also included a couple of examples of meditations, some problem solving approaches using NLP, and a starter for mind-mapping. You may want to go further in studying these methods, but these 'tasters' will give you a flavour of what power you can unlock within yourself.

Combining the techniques of meditation, NLP and mind-mapping with an awareness of the components of our intelligences, we can drastically raise our levels of consciousness and creativity. Our ability to accept the truth of our circumstances, and to see the real potential we have to affect dramatic change in ourselves enables us to make a real change in the world we inhabit. To make real change takes a set of practical goals, and an ongoing commitment, and for that, some strategies for time management are indispensable. Here are examples of simple techniques from those disciplines, things that you can do starting from right where you are.

Once you begin on this path of change, there is no limit to how far you can go.

MEDITATION

The word 'Meditation,' from the Latin *meditatio*, has three meanings: practice, exercise, both physical and mental, and preparation. The many forms of meditation, eastern and western in origin, some mystical some not, are mostly used to still or quieten the mind. Often coupled with solitude and prolonged silence, meditation can bring physical relaxation and improve concentration.

Most faiths practise meditation in some form, with varying degrees of importance, and techniques differ according to their focal point. Some direct the centre of attention to all the details of the outer world with the aim of 'mindfulness,' others focus on a specific object and this is known as a 'concentrative' meditation. Some practices oscillate between the outer world and the object.

Meditation can foster spiritual growth, when used in prayer or as a path to attain salvation and enlightenment. Meditation has also been used to improve general health; to reduce stress, to lower blood pressure and to strengthen the immune system.

Here are two meditation techniques: a breathing technique that can lead to mindfulness, and a visual technique that can lead towards greater spirituality.

The aim of meditation is to come to a place of inner stillness and clarity by turning off the inner chatter of the mind. It is usually helpful to begin by sitting in a position where you will be comfortable to remain still for a while, preferably with the spine vertical.

In each case, if a thought comes along, or an outside distraction, acknowledge it and allow it to go.

Breathing meditation. This is a breathing technique to help you reach a place of inner stillness. Counting your breath helps you to slow your mind, to a point where you find that you have stopped counting. Let your body breathe normally. This technique serves a double purpose, developing your concentration and integrating your whole being, which leads towards mindfulness.

Start by sitting comfortably with your spine as straight as possible. Close your eyes and sit quietly for a minute, and simply breathe, inhaling and exhaling slowly. When you are relaxed, begin to count your breaths, thinking quietly, 'one' on the first breath out, 'two' for the next, and so on, up to ten.

If your mind wanders into thought or to the world around you, don't worry; simply start again. Be patient, and be gentle with yourself. Practise five sets of ten breaths until you do it without effort and without being distracted, keeping your thoughts only on the breathing and counting. As a daily practice, this alone will soon have a calming effect, and your concentration will improve.

Once you feel comfortable clearing your mind with your eyes closed, begin to practise five sets of ten breaths, but this time with your eyes open, again with the aim of keeping your mind from distraction.

Be patient with yourself – don't give up. The more you practise, the more benefit you will see. The fruits of meditation are usually felt some time after you have meditated. It is worth paying attention to thoughts which come along immediately after you meditate, as this is often a time of heightened focus and creativity. Meditation also brings tremendous cumulative benefits, with changes and improvements rippling out over time.

Forgiveness meditation. Harbouring grudges, resentment and anger is a destructive energy which threatens the balance of our life. This visualisation technique on forgiveness helps us overcome our negative attitude and brings us closer to serenity.

Start by sitting comfortably and consciously. Acquaint yourself with every part of your body, by identifying it with a little movement and then relaxing it. Start with your feet and work upwards. Concentrate on your breathing; inhaling and exhaling deliberately, slowly and rhythmically.

With each in-breath, visualise yourself being filled with an energy of comfort, love and forgiveness. Inhale slowly and deeply feel how every breath cleanses you of all your grudges, resentment and anger. Hold your breath for as long as it is comfortable, and send this energy to every cell in your body, from your toes up to the crown of your head.

Breathe out slowly and deeply, visualising every physical, mental, and emotional impurity leaving your body. On each breath you take, hold and release, forgive and cleanse yourself to become pure, glowing and whole. When you see yourself as pure, visualise someone who needs your forgiveness and send them your compassion and love. Forgive them in your heart and never carry any resentment towards them ever again. Keep on breathing in, holding your breath, and breathing out again.

Now visualise someone whom you caused to suffer, and send them your healing and loving energy. Feel free from guilt for your transgression towards them. With every in-breath, take in forgiveness and with every out-breath give forgiveness, gradually coming to a place of deeper wholeness.

NEURO-LINGUISTIC PROGRAMMING

Neuro-linguistic programming is a school of thought based upon cognitive psychology which helps reconstruct the way we think. It re-examines the dynamics of how we communicate, use our senses and it influences the way we behave.

Self-exploration is encouraged through a range of techniques, including open questioning. It enables us to challenge our own attitudes, perceptions, assumptions and thought processes, also referred to as maps. By becoming aware of the way we use language, expression, intonation and how we interact with ourselves and others we can begin to see our habitual patterns. These maps can help us identify the areas of our life that are not functioning properly. It can give us greater control over our choices and patterns of behaviour. By helping us to think, act and be aware of our unconscious, NLP offers a pragmatic and effective approach to self-understanding, and the tools required to take action. The power of beliefs and values affect the very thought processes we use to find happiness and meaning. When we become aware of these internalised beliefs and how they enrich us or limit us we can adapt, change or modify them. NLP examines the way we understand and how we communicate consciously and unconsciously. It explores the power of words beyond their sounds and meanings and helps us develop dynamic thought processes which enable us to engage in more productive ways of sharing and connecting. This remodelling and transformation is the process of reconditioning our own internal programming. This mind shift revolutionises every aspect of how we function.

NLP evolved in the 1970s in the USA, through the early work of Richard Bandler and John Grinder who were influenced by the pioneers of Gestalt Therapy Fritz Perls and Virginia Satir. They in turn worked alongside Milton H Erickson. At the time many anthropological advances were made and the influence of epistemology and sociology were shaping our use of linguistics. NLP is increasingly being used in training, management and personal development. It explores the way we develop logical thought by offering new avenues of thinking because words influence everything we do, thereby coding our experiences.

Of the many methods, techniques and processes that NLP has evolved since its inception in the 1970s, let us look at two in particular: modelling and reframing.

Modelling is a method most often used to acquire skills to be successful in our working lives, by following and analysing the behaviour of somebody who possesses that skill. This enables us to distil their actions and habits to make a model or pattern for ourselves. Thus we separate and document their ability, in order to reproduce the skill in ourselves. This method can also be used to understand the patterns of our own behaviour in order to 'model' and extend the more successful parts of ourselves.

For example, you may ask yourself:
'Have I wronged or hurt anyone recently?'

Think about that event. Consider how the person you hurt may have felt. Remember how you felt afterwards. Then try to remember a similar or even identical situation where you had the same outcome without having hurt anybody. Distil this model of your own behaviour by homing in on the positive habit only.

So then, ask yourself:
'How might I transform the situation for the person I hurt?'

'How might I transform the situation for myself?'

When you may be about to hurt somebody, recall

43

your answers and use what you learned to achieve a more positive habit.

Reframing is a technique where an undesirable behaviour or situation is given a positive intention, or whereby our view of a problem is changed. It is literally re- framed. We change the way we perceive an event, and thereby change its meaning. Once the meaning changes, our responses and behaviours will also change. Reframing our behaviour, a situation or a problem by using different language, puts a different spin on how we see the world and this changes our attitude and the meaning of the problem or situation.

For example: Let us consider the prospect of hunger.

Not having enough food: for people in some parts of our world this is a serious reality. We in the developed countries are privileged that can choose to view the prospect of hunger as an opportunity to fast. We may fast for health reasons, for spiritual cleansing, or as a spiritual observance.

Faced with a task or circumstance that we don't like, we can use this technique to reframe our approach to it, finding a positive motivation in what would otherwise seem a negative situation. This can also be a means for us to gain understanding and empathy with others. Those, for instance, who don't have the same choices that we do.

MIND-MAPPING

Mind-maps are illustrated diagrams around a central topic, with sub-topics radiating outwards. Drawings, colours, icons and symbols are used to make mind-maps very visual. The technique has long been used in business and by engineers, and is increasingly popular with students. They provide a very useful way to organise information, and have some very powerful properties for us. As a way to take notes in lectures or meetings, they have the advantages of being very quick and, perhaps even more importantly, the structure provides rich memory cues.

Users of mind-maps quickly develop a personal style, and the more they practise, the more powerful their maps become, both for retaining information and for discovering unexpected connections. Mind maps are an enjoyable way to make discoveries and connections that we may otherwise overlook. They use drawing, but people who can't draw, or don't think they can, often get even more out of them than accomplished draughtspersons, because they are more open and less conditioned in art skills.

A mind-map of friends Use unlined paper, and have at least three colours of pens or pencils ready. Turn the paper landscape – long sides at the top and bottom, short sides left and right. This gives your ideas and observations room to grow.

Start with the topic of 'FRIENDS'; write the topic in big capital letters, in the centre, with a pen. Draw a shape, maybe a heart, around the topic. Write the names of friends as they occur to you, in smaller capitals around the centre. Group friends whom you would see as connected in any way, near to each other.

Draw a line in a colour from the centre out to each friend, along under the friend's name and then, on branches like a tree, write some things that particular friend means to you. Use the colours to express themes; friends from school, friends who you don't see often enough, friends with large families – anything that seems interesting or fun.

Ideas and images may occur to you. Write or draw them where they first seem appropriate, and draw branches from whoever or whatever they relate to. Look for more ways to make connections, such as friends who play musical instruments or friends who are athletic.

A mind-map should be drawn as rapidly as possible, with the minimum of conscious thought, to allow the maximum unexpected connections and observations to appear. Take any opportunity to play and have fun with drawing the map. The more fun you have, the more valuable the map will become.

Afterwards, do the same thing as you did with 'FRIENDS', but this time start with, 'NEXT YEAR', and think about your aims, dreams and ambitions.

TIME MANAGEMENT

The object of time management is to give us control of how we spend our time. Extensive use of a diary or a planner sets a discipline where all appointments are scheduled, as are almost all other activities. The more detailed your schedule, the more you will be able to pack into your day and the more you will get out of it. Marking out a formal time for your goals and aims ensures that things like meditation and spending time in reflection do not get squeezed out or sidelined. Time management reduces procrastination, and it enables us to review how effectively we actually use our time.

Start here This book should spark a number of ideas for you to pursue. Use a diary or a planner to make definite time for putting them into practice. The first step is creating the intentions, but it is vital to carry through, and put your intentions into practise. Throughout the book, at the ends of most chapters, are some questions for you to consider. Have a pad or notebook handy, and write your answers to the questions quickly, don't think about them. Your instinctive reaction is most revealing, and you may be surprised by some of your answers as you re-read them later. Date your answers and keep them for future reference – the record of your journey will be a source of learning and inspiration. Some questions are repeated, and over time your answers may change.

PUTTING IT ALL TOGETHER

At the end of each chapter is a list of topics for you to explore, through meditation and by self examination. Dedicate regular, quiet time to practise meditation and make discoveries about yourself and your progress. Use the topics to meditate and explore your intelligences. When you discover changes that you want to make, use the NLP techniques to help you bring the changes about. Use mind-mapping to explore relationships and situations, and employ time-management to keep your progress on track.

Ask yourself:
What makes me happy?

Do my actions match my values?

How does happiness fit into my goals?

Some topics for meditation:
The Breathing meditation (on page 38)

The Forgiveness meditation (on page 40)

IN SEARCH OF HAPPINESS

Happiness comes from within us, not from what's outside. Distractions, discontent and preconceptions are what separate us from happiness

Happiness is not something that we can find, it is something that we are, something we create within ourselves. It is a state of being, a consciousness, a way of perceiving and knowing. It is the way we choose to see the world despite itself. Only when we understand this can we live it.

The desire for happiness drives and motivates most of us. All too often we get trapped in what we do to find happiness, and lose sight of what happiness really is. We become so occupied with survival and the rush of modern life that we fail to recognise what gives us meaning.

A friend's son was leaving for university, and pointed out that they had not talked in over a year. In that time he had experimented with drugs, got into debt, had a serious relationship, performed two public concerts and won an art prize. All this was *This power is within you now. If you choose to use it, you will be changed forever.* new to my friend who had been too busy providing material support to his family, but was not present in their lives. No one was more saddened or surprised than my friend, realising that he had become the very person he had hated - his own father who was never home.

Mystics and prophets offer different paths to a wisdom which answers the same questions. Springing from the same passions, it is illuminated by the same fires. Whether Sioux or Mongolian hill-tribesman, Wall-Street trader or Maasai warrior, there are things that bind us so deeply together that we speak with one tongue and have but one desire in our hearts.

Delight is so obvious that we often miss it. Being

here is as simple as that, it is about actually 'being' here in this now, sharing this joy, not working for a joy somewhere in the future. Loving those around us is being in their creativity, in the process of total involvement with life, all life. It is never too late to start, never to late to forgive, to create.

> *Creativity requires the courage to let*
> *go of certainties.*
>
> Erich Fromm

Joy may come with a prayer or a book, but it doesn't come *from* the prayer or the book. Take a book or a printed prayer and shake it. See if any joy falls out. The joy comes from within the reader. For sure, it was the writer or artist who put joy into a book, a prayer, a CD or a painting, but it remains there, flat and lifeless, until a new eye surprises it out. We can learn to create joy for ourselves and determine the quality of our lives. That is as close as any of us can come to being happy. Being fully involved with and engaged in what we are doing, we can shape our own destiny, guided by the soft whisper of our hearts.

When we are aware of every detail in our lives we develop a deep sense of self-comprehension and personal insight that gives us spiritual and emotional intelligence. Whether we are happy depends on inner harmony, not on the controls we are able to exert over the forces of the universe. With this insight we can experience things with deeper intensity. Every single thing that happens is realised with a fresh awakening, nothing is taken for granted.

For each of us there are thousands of opportunities every day, exciting challenges to expand ourselves. Everything we experience - joy or pain, interest or boredom - registers in the mind as information. If we take control of the information, we can choose how our lives will be. This power is within you now, and if you choose to use it, you will be changed forever; this is the simplest and most powerful mind transformation you can make; to choose how you perceive what is around you.

Happiness is experienced in different ways by different people, but the raw experience is intrinsically the same. While we all might look for it differently, it usually turns up in the same place. The state we refer to as happiness is that sensation and awareness in which everything is in balance. It may not be euphoric, it might be

We get trapped in what we do to find happiness, and lose sight of what happiness really is.

deeply still, but it is a personal awareness that 'this is it.' This relatively rare experience seems to be the most common desire for us all, 'I want to be happy.' Much of our lives is spent in pursuit of this often illusive state of consciousness. I suspect that the path to happiness is infinitely more accessible than we suppose. The more we can let go the trivia that drains our waking day, distracting us from our inner voice, the more often we have the 'optimal experience.'

Some time ago I was in a small, run-down hospital in Mogadishu with children whose legs had been blown off by land mines. There were two children to each single bed, the mattresses were torn, there were no sheets, no electricity and no curtains. The hospital generator had been stolen along with the hospital gates months before. There was in fact very little of anything except a lot of laughter, a lot of goodness and a lot of hope. I had first visited the wards over twenty years ago during a drought, but this time the children were the victims of war and violence. In playing with the children and talking to the nurses I found two things; a great sense of care for each other and interest in the needs of the other, and an energy of calm and welcome. There was nothing, yet there was everything, absolutely nothing in its most literal sense, but ultimately, everything.

Inner joy lives here in the now, and in the temple of our hearts. By stretching ourselves, by reaching towards higher challenges, we become increasingly extraordinary individuals. It is how we respond to stress that determines whether we will profit from misfortune or be miserable.

In a supermarket in the UK I watched a couple pushing a heavily laden shopping trolley. Beautifully dressed and in their forties, they were in the midst of a fierce argument about deserts. The man stormed off amid remarks that could only have wounded them both further. Later I saw two old ladies with faces like maps, wrinkled by laughter and worn by work. They bantered and joked as they shuffled down an aisle of vegetables discussing whether they should have potatoes with carrots or peas. They bought the smallest bag of potatoes and two carrots. Every day we see people who can teach us, if we have our eyes open.

Life is often difficult and painful. Change too can be hard. The familiar is always more comfortable.

The ways we interact, our habitual expressions and phrases, the image we project, are reflections of what is inside us. If we project negative perceptions and attitudes, it is likely that we are not at peace, not delighted by what life has offered to us. If we use positive, supportive language we are likely to be happier and more effective. Each of us has a picture, however vague, of what we would like to accomplish before we die. How close we get to attaining this goal becomes the measure for the quality of our lives. If it remains beyond reach, we grow resentful or resigned; if it is at least in part achieved, we experience a sense of happiness and satisfaction.

Problems arise when people are so fixated on what they want to achieve that they cease to derive pleasure from the present. When that happens, they forfeit their chances of contentment. The roots of the discontent are internal, and each person must disentangle them personally, with his or her own power.

Creating inner experience requires a drastic change in attitude about what is important and what is not. That is the secret of changing ourselves and the secret of becoming who we want to be. The world possesses already a lot of wisdom from which we can learn, a lot of insight that can make our journey easier. Finding wonder and joy, delight and pleasure in everything we do is an art, a very simple and powerful way of living. The reason so few people practise the art of happiness is because they would have to unlearn ways of thinking and doing that are the habits of a lifetime. We form opinions and then spend our entire lives validating what we believe to be true. This rigidity is sad, because there is so much we can learn from points of view that are different from our own. We sometimes disturb the spirit within us with worries that do not help us move forward. Life is often difficult and painful, change too can be very hard, the familiar is always more comfortable.

Happiness comes when we engage with the world as it is, letting go of illusions and preconceptions about how it should be. When volunteers come to Africa, they often think that they are open minded and ready to listen to the cultures of others. So often, however, they bring thought cycles that limit their ability to listen. Confronted with whole world views alien to their own, they start processes of comparison, defining differences and identifying failure. By not being open to entirely different constructions of reality, we prevent ourselves from learning at a very basic level. For those who are able to learn and listen and who are awake to radically different ways of life, there is illumination with ever evolving fresh possibilities. This starts in the minutiae of how we begin to form opinions, assumptions, guesses and ideas. It is this intrinsic set of perceptions and attitude-forming sparks that are critical in resetting our minds so that we can think openly.

There is a strange type of dream in which you find yourself eating - have you ever had one? Though you eat in the dream, the food somehow does not fill you or take away your hunger. And the distress wakes you and you go downstairs and make toast. How long do we have to dream of consuming happiness before we wake up and act?

The way we live is conditioned by the energies around us, if we allow them that power.

A rather joyless person I know discussed the difference between joy and happiness. 'Joy,' she said, 'is spiritual. You can be happy drinking a glass of water when you are thirsty.' But, but, I thought... I had this wonderful image of the days when I rode my bike over the remote mountains of Europe, remembering how wonderful it was to stop on a hot mountain road, take out the water bottle and drink, how beautiful the water looked in the sunlight. I do not see that there can be a distinction. A bottle of tepid water in the heat of the day or a cup of coffee on your desk, each holds the possibility of connecting you with the limitless. It's not so much believing that happiness lies outside us that is the trouble, it is the belief that we must get the happiness into ourselves, consume or possess it in some way. It is the 'out there-ness' of happiness that we find hard to tolerate. If we cannot possess things, we grow nervous that they will flit away. We want control and we cannot have it.

Happiness is not something that you can control.

> **Ask yourself:**
> *What things does my happiness presently depend upon?*
>
> *Which people does my happiness presently depend upon?*
>
> *What makes me happy?*
>
> *When will I next dance?*
>
> **A topic for meditation:**
> *What brings me joy.*

Before dawn Ireneus awoke drenched in sweat, his sleep disturbed once more. A girl slept easily at his side, exhausted from his tenderness, intoxicated by his beauty. He was blessed. Blessed with work that saw him prosper, humour that drew him company, wealth enough to buy fabulous clothes, the best of wines and homes in great cities. He had danced through the night again, he had laughed and played, drunk his fill. Something within him was disquiet and grew dissatisfied. Those who shared his delight and pleasured in his company, eased his mind. His friends bade him forget imaginings and venture more with them. Together they found new beauty, great markets and new places, and in time the newness distracted him for a while.

The way we live

Distractions are often a way of avoiding the things we know we need to deal with. Meditation, self-knowledge and calm help us reduce distraction, and focus our energy

How we are as we get out of bed in the morning is what we carry in our minds during the day. How we walk, how we speak, how we listen, how we hold on to things and how we let things go start from how we greet the day. Our way of life has a lot to do with our attitude and our opinion, our inner joy and our laughter, how we deal with stress and how we deal with the surprises life pitches at us. The way we live is conditioned by the energies around us, if we allow them that power. Western lifestyles are driven by materialism and consumerism. Dr Carol Craig said, 'We are a culture that encourages feelings of lack of self-worth. We're a culture that goes out of its way to make sure people don't feel good about themselves.' It is a culture that fuels self-rejection not self-celebration. It depends on dissatisfaction and an insatiable desire to fuel the consumer economy. Inner contentment can almost be an act of rebellion.

We are rarely at ease. We are taught that we must produce and earn, we must succeed and prosper, and we cannot slow down, so we run. We are often in a struggle with what we have and what we want. Our society identifies success with owning more, having more, acquiring more. We are taught to get more. We live in a world driven by the engines of get, have, own, buy, earn, produce more, more, more. This 'more' is stuff, houses and cars, clothes and gadgets, technology and possessions. As Erich Fromm reflected, 'If I am what I have and if I lose what I have, who then am I?' The pressure of modern life to accumulate things drains our energy, steals our sense of self and diminishes us.

Many cultures embrace the unknown and do not feel compelled to have answers for everything.

A colleague once complained that he never had any time for himself. His children consumed all his free time, his job absorbed his weekends and he had no personal space. Frank was overweight, tired all the time, trapped by responsibilities. He resented the demands that everyone placed on him. Frank was so busy that it was only after three rescheduled meetings that we finally sat down. He was half an hour late, and arrived agitated and panting. The traffic was bad and the London Underground was running late. Frank sat down and ordered a large coffee and almond croissant.

As he moaned about the crowded coffee shop and uncomfortable seats, he told me he could not stay long because he had to get home early to sort out the kids. In the first five minutes he had made sixteen negative statements and blamed kids, waitresses, London Transport and his secretary for some of the hassles that had plagued his afternoon.

I suggested to Frank that he make a list of all the things that were bothering him and the reasons why he felt stressed. It was a long list. When asked to describe his average day, it was a series of pressured tasks, deadlines and duties. He was very, very busy being busy. The reality was somewhat different, his frenetic behaviour caused him to achieve little, be late for everything and fight with those around him. Frank was angry with himself, frustrated that nothing seemed to be manageable and tired with those around him who seemed to be having an easier life. At forty five Frank was struggling to keep up with younger, fitter, sharper managers in his office. Frank was not only stressed, he was burnt out.

When we are stuck in this kind of behaviour our thought cycles become locked and while we are able to talk about our anxieties, we are often unwilling to break the pattern that create the problem. Change in these situations is difficult. I left Frank to think about the lists he had written and suggested that he kept a log of his thoughts and conversations. I also asked his wife, an old friend, to do the same, simply to keep track of the positive and negative. A couple of weeks later, we met again and Frank was tired and lethargic as usual. After an hour's conversation I asked him how positive he thought he was. He felt that he was generally optimistic and supportive of those close to him. His wife, who was sitting beside me, smiled. I played back to him our conversation of the past hour, which had been mostly general chit chat. Within the course of one hour Frank had made about one hundred and forty two negative remarks. It was a subconscious expression of his interpretation of life. Like many people, Frank's real problem was not time management but self management, his crisis was not that he had no space for himself but that he was trapped

We have to put our lives behind what we really believe, otherwise it is only words.

within himself. The cause of Frank's anxieties were not external but within his own mind.

Over the following year, he learned to trust his children more and more, talking to them with respect and treating them as adults. He started IT training programmes, joined a tennis club and watched less TV. In time his sleep improved, he ate better, lost weight, and became calmer. Frank was beginning to find awareness, take control of his inner experience and take responsibility for himself without blaming others. Only once we have started to listen to the voice within can we pay attention to the needs and personalities of those we love.

Our hyperactive culture trains us to be frenetic and dissatisfied. We are in a state of constant distraction. I know people who are plugged in to some device from the moment they wake up in the morning to the moment they go to sleep at night. From the alarm clock and morning television, MP3 players and car radio, there is a stream of external noise. Work is a rush to keep pace with e-mails, meetings, phone calls and deadlines. Lunch is caught on the run, juggling text messages and mobile phone calls, and the rest of the day is more work. Ever more stressful journeys home seem to take ever longer, then we are often too tired to do much more than domestic chores, slumping finally with microwaved food in front of the T.V. before falling asleep. Each decade our culture depends more on information technology, with many people so hooked to mobile phones and the internet that they feel deprived without them. This information overload generates a continuous rush that is harmful to us. Technology pours so much information, news and stimulation into our day that our senses are rarely left in quietness. A laptop in 2007 has more computer power than all the world's computers in 1967 combined. We are a generation who fear missing something if we turn anything off.

Popular media mashes everything down to opinion, speculation and gossip. Everything is either good or bad, and all too often what makes the news is bad. Media creates heroes and villains. The constant demand for answers reduces everything to the lowest common denominator; a box to put the answer in. 'Either-or'

Anxiety, stress disorders, nutritional problems and depression are endemic in our society.

thinking dominates Western thought. David Beckham is either good or bad, Mother Teresa was either a Saint or a tyrant. You are either 'with us' or 'against us.' This black and white thinking stains how we see ourselves and each other. We must have careers, must have jobs, and must live within our limits. Originality has become deviant in a kind of Big Brother society that promotes sameness and discourages creative diversity. This diminishes us. It restricts our scope to think for ourselves. To nurture originality and our own thoughts, we must challenge the assumptions and patterns to which we have been conditioned since birth. Nothing is healthier than to shatter the moulds.

Not every society thinks this way. Many cultures embrace the unknown and do not feel compelled to have answers for everything. Our compulsion to analyse, count and want to know everything often creates deep anxieties. People that I have worked with over the years have taught me a great deal about enjoying life. Many of the reflections in this book are from the lives of people who are deeply and profoundly happy. They are people who are able to find harmony and balance despite everything else, and the lessons of such lives can only benefit us.

Here is the first real step forward: choice.

Many people yearn for something more. A young college student named Valerie said, 'What do I want in life? Good question.... People here seem empty, and as one might expect to find in an Ivy League institution, they are concerned with fitting into the pattern; succeed and get wonderful paying jobs. People talk a lot about what touches them; children starving, AIDS, global warming, etc., but in the end no one gets really involved.' Like so many people searching, she said, 'When I was a child, I wanted to save dolphins, and yet sometimes I just wonder if by myself I will be able to make a difference. Somehow I know that I am still the saviour of dolphins more than anything else ...we keep on following our normal lives... if people could act more than they talked, it would be awesome... but for now, that is all I am able to do. One day, though, I hope this will in some way or another change.' Where change can begin, in a practical way? That is the question. Right now, is the answer.

We try to live as best we can, we try to make time for the things that really matter to us. I have often found myself failing to do the things I want to do, the things that matter. I sometimes get caught up in the unimportant stuff. I remember thinking a great deal about the gulf between the rich and poor, I remember arguing with friends about the need to change the way we live. I felt angry on behalf of the poor, I felt incensed about the greed of the rich and the apathy of the middle class. I quoted statistics and facts, and a lot of opinion. Not one child was ever healed by argument, not one mother was fed by my anger and not one mind improved by my indignation. There was not a single human being who had been helped by the statistics on my lips, not one tear wiped away by my pity.

In reflecting on the things I had said, I noticed the gap between what I was saying and doing. There was a lot of rhetoric, but very little practice. If I felt so strongly and believed so deeply, what was I doing about the things I was so concerned about? We have to put our lives behind what we really believe otherwise it is only words. I was living in a comfortable capital city in Europe, talking of the struggle of the poor in the slums. I was skiing in beautiful ski resorts chatting about a better world. The way I was living my life did not relate to what I believed. I ended up leaving my life of very real privilege and setting off to find the poorest people I had been talking about. I wanted to see for myself and learn. I am still learning nearly thirty years later and most of my time is spent in the Sub-Sahara with people hoping for a better tomorrow.

In relationships, too, the things we say and promise are rarely the realities we bring to each other. What we profess is often one thing and what we do is something very different. Becoming our true selves involves accepting this about ourselves. It is not about judging ourselves; it is about listening to our inner voice, and learning from the way we do things. So often in relationships, we can use the love someone has for us to manipulate them. Love can so often be a weapon.

It is often challenging to find meaningful time for those we love, time to unravel ourselves from the day's demands and let go. In a nine to five perform-ance-centred culture people become part of the rush-hour tidal wave, trapped in the 'have to' stuff. It is no wonder that anxiety, stress disorders, nutri-tional problems and depression are endemic in our society. It is inevitable that alienation and distress are increasing, and it's no surprise that our children feel frustrated and lost.

My greatest failures may have been in taking those I love for granted, in failing to invest the time and energy in sensing and listening to the unspoken. Most communication is invisible and unheard; it often passes unnoticed in the imperceptible fabric of relationships. So often we fail to be aware of or tuned-in to these inaudible voices.

People write to me, from every possible background. Many are teenagers struggling to find their way in a world where they are pressured to perform and produce. Others have relationships and jobs that challenge and fulfil them, others are unemployed or ill. What these people have in common is a desire to celebrate life, realise their gifts and become fully alive. The hundreds of letters and e-mails communicate concerns and frustrations. So much anxiety stems from the feeling

Children naturally think of themselves as beautiful and terribly important.

many people have of being trapped, limited or imprisoned by the constraints of modern life. Far from liberating us, our high-speed lifestyles often leave us drained and exhausted. We are often left with a profound sense that we ought to be living differently. We all have a gut feeling about what we are looking for in the day-to-day adventure of our lives.

My friend David is thoughtful and gracious, he is popular, and others are drawn to him. He came from South Africa to London with innocence and a purity of heart. I asked him what he wanted out of life, and he replied, '... I want to give back... I want to have friends around me whom I love... I want to have a good relationship with my family... I want to know the world... I want to connect with people... to understand why we do what we do...' David went on to explain, 'I want to know what makes us behave the way we do... why some people can see the truth in things... why others can't... how do you learn to see through the barriers... through the layers... why are we so guarded... most of us haven't been hurt badly enough to be this way...so why are we so cold? Why are we so afraid of saying things with honesty... looking at people and saying what we feel?' He asked, 'Is it our fear of rejection? I think we live in a society where people love to see failure sometimes, they are weaned on bad news... it is almost as if they love to see a loser... why is that? Why don't we celebrate what is good and true anymore?' I asked David what made him sad. 'I think we form judgements before we even know the truth... and that preconception we have of someone, ultimately affects how we interact with them... which was false to begin with so we close doors all the time.

'I think it was people, moving to a large city... where everyone seemed so perfect on the outside... but so flawed on the inside... but it is the outside you see first... and you build your opinions on that... and when you are young... you often don't know better. You strive to look like the guy with the nice clothes or the fantastic body... but really, those things don't last, do they? They live for the high of today... an instant hit... and it's so destructive... They can't find beauty in the simple things... conversations... the ocean... life... trust...'

The way we choose to live is so often influenced by our peer groups and the opinions of others. While these influences can often be positive, they can also diminish us or lower our self esteem, sometimes even extinguishing our light. Here is the first real step forward: choice.

Once we create within our daily lives the happiness which we all deserve, our whole outlook and attitude to life will change. We will practise new habits, dynamic expansive ways of thinking, we will begin to realise and live our inner dreams. We will discover hidden wisdom and explore our many unused talents. Through channelling these energies we will awaken a new self, a self that sees through different eyes. Eventually we will get into a wonderful habit of not being upset when things go wrong. No one can reveal to us anything which does not already lie half awake within our hearts.

Many people argue, are confrontational, and fight over practically everything, turning their lives into a series of battles over relatively small stuff. Negative thinking drains us and creates darkness where there is light. When we are in a bad mood, we have little perspective and we are easily hurt. The strange thing is that it is we who hurt ourselves the most in our lives. Modern life can be exhausting, usually because we are deprived and starved of stillness, wonder, sleep and mystery which is what we all crave. To be without these things is emotional anorexia. We become too stressed by it all.

Self-worth cannot be instilled by others. You are worthy because you say it is so. If you depended on others for your value it would be other-worth.

Changing the way you think or feel or live is possible but never easy. Children just naturally think of themselves as beautiful and terribly important, but as adults it is not helpful to be so self-centred. Once you recognise just how good you are, you won't need others to reinforce your value or values by making them conform to your diktats. It is so amazing, how great people really are. Every one is magic.

> *Life is far too important to be taken seriously.*
>
> Oscar Wilde

Ronán's father had the habit, everywhere there was water deeper enough, he would have to get in and swim. Impervious to cold, he could swim in stuff that was close to freezing. Wicklow Mountain streams, the touch of which would stop the heart of an ox - no problem. He floated, delighted, in the dark brown water. Not Ronán, though - he suffered terrible pains in the wrists and ankles in cold water. Which made it all the more strange that he too felt the need to swim, exactly as his father did.

'As I waded into a small bay in Kerry, I realised that the water was cold, that I would soon be freezing, and that I could not understand why the hell I felt obliged to go swimming. But I knew, too, that in a few minutes I would be out there in the middle of the little bay, watching the setting sun on the hills opposite, floating on my back, enjoying the gracefulness that water confers on us clumsy people, and I realised something about my father; he didn't invent this compulsion to go swimming. It was the other way around - there was a swimming gene which had my father so that it, the gene, could go swimming, and because it wanted the adventure to go on and on, it had me too. This gene has been around perhaps since forever, slipping from person to person along the aeons, animating each one of us with this wild delight in buoyancy, this love of water and swimming. And this was when, in the middle of a bay in Kerry, I realised that life had me, that life had plans for me, that life was one endless adventure, that life had given me the amazing invitation to join in.'

Sometimes you make important realisations when thinking about very unimportant things. I have a strong sense of this from the Maasai. That life is

The Western mind has difficulty thinking beyond its own experience

endless, and everyone is invited. We often go through life missing the big picture. The way we live comes not in neatly packaged book chapters but as points of conflict, at random, in kicks and jolts. The petty argument, the headache, the kiss, the toothache, the party, the gift, the stunning moon over the city and the tragedy in a far off country. These are the things that make up our world along with the stale corn-flakes, the song that makes us cry, pop-up porn and a call from a long lost friend.

73

> *Many people know so little about*
> *what is beyond their short range of*
> *experience. They look within*
> *themselves - and find nothing.*
> *Therefore they conclude that there is*
> *nothing outside themselves either.*

Helen Keller

Growing and becoming is about exploring, learning and creating, it is about challenging ourselves. Every day is full of possibilities and choices about how we can respond. Every hour is a gateway to change, a fresh opportunity to live with new choices seen with new eyes. The way we live is woven from what we do, what drives us, the wisdom we possess, the way we are, the aspirations we pursue and the intelligence we use to make sense of it all.

Ask yourself:
Am I gentle with myself?

Do I take time out for those around me?

Am I in charge of my schedule?

A topic for meditation:
My choices.

The way we are

*We can learn and practise for what we want more
of – and un-learn for what we want less of*

We are habitual creatures, eager for the familiar and uneasy with the unknown. Once we hit adulthood many of us relax into the habitual grooves we have established for ourselves, rarely questioning how we live, how we reach decisions, or how we think about problems. When we think of habits we usually think of how we drink, smoke, bite our nails or sleep, but not the things that underlie our actions. The conditioning we receive in childhood often predetermines our later behaviour.

The Maasai are known for their stoic self-discipline and Spartan lifestyle. Problems are not really part of their way of thinking. Westerners tend to face the needs and challenges of poverty with agendas, time plans, assessments, strategies and priorities. Projects brought to the Maasai, come and go, tied to timetables and well-meaning donors. Many white people leave after their volunteer assignments with the Maasai, frustrated and perplexed at the seeming lack of enthusiasm. I have often looked at the two cultural mind sets and been saddened by people's inability to comprehend a different way of seeing things.

The Maasai do not grasp the need to do things in the Western aid agencies' narrow limitations. Donors often have no reference point for a view that does not leap at their model of progress. The Western mind has difficulty thinking beyond its own experience or accepting other ways of interpreting development.

For over twenty-five years I have worked closely with Sarune. Like his father, Sarune is calm and serene, soft spoken and gentle. His disposition and customs lead him to approach every drama and crisis, accident and need, with tranquillity and peace which immediately restructure every situation. He has an internal balance that calms the anxiety of others, not through words but through presence. Those who meet him often ask what it is within him that generates such serenity; part of the answer lies in

When negative thoughts invade your mind, break the pattern and replace them with something more worthy.

his acquired habit of self-possession, the habit of self-presence and the habit of not letting those around him change his own inner calm.

We all have our habitual approaches to situations, our stock responses to daily drama. Our friends know how we behave if they are late, how we feel when we are hurt, what we say when we are angry or when we are drunk. The more we know someone, the more we learn to read the unspoken communication in their tone, their body, their silence and their manner. I have a friend who becomes very quiet and calm when he is happy, and extrovert and manic when he is anxious. Another who is quiet when sad, and exuberant when elated. People are different, and the more we move in other cultures, the more the complexity deepens as different societies have different norms and expectations, other expressions and rules of social engagement and sharing.

We have not only our personal habits, but also deeply etched behaviours from the cultures in which we were socialised. A challenge for visitors to tribal communities in Africa is to respect the social norms of their culture.

We learn through our mistakes in life, and hopefully even re-educate ourselves with habits we consider good. Neuro-linguistic programming, which we introduced earlier, offers powerful ways to help us do this. When your instincts fail to read the cultural habits of the place you are in, your own actions may be misconstrued or distorted. We should always try to learn the social dynamics of any group we engage with before expressing ourselves openly. In India this might mean understanding the protocols of individual behaviour. In Africa it might mean knowing who speaks and sits where and when in a village meeting; while in Europe it might mean grasping the diverse politically correct sensitivities of a group. In every situation we should try to understand the complex balance of the habits of the group and our own behaviour before engaging with them.

Becoming conscious of the habits, internal and external, private and public that pervade our lives, we can begin to improve the way we are.

Do you notice how you listen to people, how you pay attention, whether you maintain eye contact when someone speaks to you? Think about how you sit, how you stand, how you hold or hang your head, or tense your shoulders. These are powerful habits; they can communicate a great deal. How do we make choices, challenge opinions, arrive at conclusions or discuss a point among friends? How we arrive at views and understand relationships and the people around us is significant. The more we examine, the more we will see repetitive patterns. We all

Catch yourself when you fall into the habit of insisting things should be other than they are.

react, respond, think and handle information, following habits we retain from previous experience. It is valuable to challenge ourselves in the ways that we address the world as it unfolds around us.

We need to ask ourselves why particular things take our attention, and need to see if we are being as true to ourselves as we could be. Too often the power within is obscured by the survival and maintenance stuff. We need to learn new responses, and to see difficulties with a different insight.

We often go from drama to drama.

We can alter our lives by altering our attitude, change every moment by the smallest shift in how we interpret what we encounter. People ask how I cope working in famines and droughts, and dealing with epidemics. In my experience, people who do such work rarely waste time over how awful things are, but just get on with the job in hand.

Complaining is a habit, and we don't always notice that we are doing it.

Some time ago I caught myself thinking how horrible the weather was in Ireland. I was driving along the canal in Dublin on a cold afternoon, and the rain was bucketing down. I was on my way to prepare a lecture, and I felt pressed for time with a long task list and pressing deadlines. As I putted along, the noise of the windscreen wipers hammering in my ears, the radio played Händel's *Lascia ch'io pianga*. I pulled the car over as the rain became heavy and I closed my eyes, letting the magic of the music touch me. When I opened my eyes again, there was no complaint in me as I looked towards the canal. I did not see how dirty it was, I barely registered the

> *When we encounter raw, undiluted pleasure living within a person, it has an amazing impact on us.*

shopping trolley or the empty beer bottles. I did not think of the cold wet windy weather that rocked my rusty Renault 4. Floating serene along the canal were swans. I got out of the car and perched on a park bench, transfixed by the tranquillity and beauty, the perfection of the moment. Here was nature incarnate. I could easily have missed the magic, but here it was, and the totality of the moment sent shivers through me. The majesty that touched me has taught me a new habit. Whenever in a hurry, stop. When negative thoughts invade your mind, break the pattern and replace the complaint or the groan with something more worthy.

Any moment can be transformed by meditation, as this one was for me.

Old habits don't always serve us well. When we are immobilised by minor obstacles, our reactions not only frustrate us but actually get in the way of solving the problem. We can be derailed by the countless distractions and anxieties, and opt for survival and escapism rather than seeking new positive possibilities. We feed on our own emotions and we surround ourselves with people of similar energies. You can see a collective anxiety in students before exams, often feeding stress to one another.

I once visited a young girl who had been hurt when bandits raided her village's cattle. A villager was killed, a bandit shot and the young girl wounded by an arrow. She was trying to recover, and one of our counsellors had asked me to talk to her family as I spoke Samburu. In the family I sensed an anger and a rage which was infectious. Everyone was looking for vengeance, everyone was angry and wanted to hunt down the bandits. The grandmother had malaria and had not slept; the men had been drinking; and the young girl's wound was not healing. During the night, I pointed out that the family needed to sleep, the men should repair the broken fences, and that there was little to be gained going after heavily armed rustlers with spears. One young man shouted that they should take revenge on the killers, even though the villager who died was killed by stampeding cattle, and the girl had been hit by a Samburu arrow, not a bullet. Their clamour for revenge had drowned out their instincts for survival and recovery. Just as a Jerry Springer audience shouts as one, so too can a community be motivated by emotions.

We often moan or complain, and usually the more we have the more we complain. Catch yourself when you fall into the habit of insisting that things should be other than they are. We do this countless times a day, waiting for a bus, lining up in the supermarket behind a really slow-moving queue. When you are at peace inside yourself, outside demands don't drain your energy from your life force. Places can often generate their own energy. Much of my time is spent in remote villages in rural Africa and Asia where the local people have little but nevertheless rarely complain. Yet in places like London, Paris or other big cities people are caught up in a frenetic motion that generates its own set of chain reactions and gives way to a more prevalent mood of complaining.

Instead of complaining, we can set ourselves the personal goal of complimenting those around us.

Stress can make us panic, make us think in circles of mounting anxiety. One thought leads to another, and another, and we become more and more agitated. By identifying the early signs, we can break the cycle and unlearn the habits. We can replace the pattern with thoughts that lead to calm and calmer. The choice can be ours if we take it.

We can unlearn negative habits by repeatedly reconditioning ourselves. This does not require mystical techniques but simple behavioural conditioning and NLP, repeating positive actions and positive words as well as training ourselves to restructure the way we think. It is hard to change how we think, but we become conscious of our habits, we can improve them.

Thoughts determine our actions, actions create habits, and habits change us. The changes shape our personality and that personality forms our future. We can replace old habits of reaction with new habits of perspective. It is impossible to feel peaceful with our heads full of concerns and annoyances. We have the choice to fill our heads with things that will calm us. Criticism, like swearing, is actually nothing more than a bad habit. Entirely different realities emerge depending on how our energy is invested in making these critical choices.

> *Such as are your habitual thoughts,*
> *such also will be the character of*
> *your mind, for the soul is dyed by*
> *the thoughts.*

> Marcus Aurelius

We all need sign posts, people in our lives who point the way a little; it is so easy to get lost without a light. We need role models.

Elle is a Kenyan who works with children who are very ill with AIDS. Elle brings laughter and light wherever he goes. Like some beacon of light he is completely self-possessed. He works with children who are so poor that many have never had a full meal. They have never sat in a chair or worn socks, never had sweets, never slept in a bed. These children have fallen over the edge into the 'underworld' that takes the lives of 50,000 children a day. The 'statistics' are children with hopes and dreams, giggles and tears. Each child is a bundle of wonder, each with vast potential. Elle works in communities hit by drought, endemic disease, hunger and AIDS. Elle is 24 and brings to each day a primordial delight in being here. No matter how grim or busy the situation, within moments someone is transformed, touched by Elle. His laughter is infectious, and his inner delight is unstoppable. When we encounter raw undiluted pleasure living within a person, it has an amazing impact on us. Even when Elle was a small boy playing in the village, he had within him that pre-grasp, that connection to the current. Anyone who has spent time in rural Africa can relate to the energy and delight that lives in the hearts of the people.

Another African friend, Patrick, will soon be setting up HIV programmes in South Africa. Patrick is an osteopath and I have known him for many years. Nothing is a problem, least of all a crisis - it is an opportunity. Patrick homes in on the delicious, the productive, and the opportunity. Natural problem-solvers are positive people who light up those

We learn through our mistakes, and hopefully re-educate ourselves with habits we consider good.

around them with pleasure, calm and delight. I have seen Patrick cope with many situations that would distress and overwhelm others, but his perception of an event is, 'What do I see that I can improve here?' He does not take the bait in an argument or partici- pate in collective opinion. His habitual reflex is to choose thoughts at a given moment which will deter- mine peace of mind and resolution, not stress. It is a choice to respond that way. This is how the decisions and actions we take at any moment create our mood and make our future. Patrick concentrates on the person who is with him. His phone is always on 'silent,' he makes people feel valuable and is plugged into them where they are at that time, without judge- ment or assumption.

When you meet Patrick there are few façades; he negotiates the feelings of anxiety and pressure we all have occasionally with the humour they deserve. Patrick behaves as he feels in his heart, and that makes him an awesome friend. It takes no talent, brains, or character to criticise, and to criticise is a habit. It is easy to demean, diminish, pull down. In Ireland we have an expression 'to slag' which means to deride or to knock. It is often done in the name of humour, but in time it wears away people's confi- dence, self esteem and sense of themselves. It can be anything from a smiling quip to overt bullying, it can be a smart retort or a sharp comment. These are all habitual practices just like swearing or complaining. Once we become aware of them there is a lot we can do to change them.

If habits are things we do all the time, we can turn bad routines into useful ones. Instead of drinking three pints of beer a night, we can drink one and two pints of water. Instead of complaining, we can set ourselves the personal goal of complimenting those around us. I know a lot of people who never say anything nice about anyone at all, ever. But I also know people like Tim Bourke. Tim is the kind of person who makes you feel proud to be human. Over the years Tim has been conned and cheated. In the Ireland of the Celtic Tiger, fuelled on obsession with money, people like Tim are slaughtered. Whatever the circumstances, no matter how bad people have been, I have never heard Tim say an unkind word about anyone behind their back. When most of us would be enraged, Tim has been gracious, when I was furious, he was tender, and when I was impatient, he was polite. He responds this way because his nature and essence is gentle and kind, his actions and words betray only that

From an early age we may have been told we cannot and we should not, but we can and we should.

character, his habitual self is kind. We can analyse these things too much or we can learn from them. We can learn from the Elles in our lives, be touched by the Patricks and grow through knowing them. Rather than say that is how Tim is, maybe we too can develop dynamic responses to life.

Thoreau said, 'The cost of a thing is the amount of

what I call life which is required to be exchanged for it, immediately or in the long run.' All too often the amount of life energy and personal energy we pay for the rat race bankrupts us to the point we forget the nature of living and the power that lies unused within us. We should do nothing in life unless we can pour our hearts into it. If we are to celebrate life and experience raw joy and undiluted happiness, a great place to begin, is to ask ourselves what we are look-ing for in our lives, what are our hopes, our visions, our dreams.

Ask yourself:
Can I identify habitual responses in others?

Can I identify habitual responses in myself?

In a glass is half as much wine as it can hold. Is the glass half empty or half full?

In the next few days, solve a crossword. If you already do crosswords, try a harder one than usual.

A topic for meditation:
I can live my dreams. I can make 'some day,' today.

Living the dream

*You don't own your life – it owns you. Your
dreams are the map it provides to guide you*

The more we are aware, the clearer the
world becomes. It is in this awareness
that our dreams live and grow. The
dreams I mean are not fleeting fragmented fantasies or clouded recollections, they are
the fires in the citadel of our souls, they are those
lights we know to be within our highest self, the
power of our whole self to be fully alive.

We can sometimes feel lost or confused in a place
that has so many pressures and demands. Discovering
our place in the fast expensive society of today can be
a lonely experience, but it need not to be. We must
celebrate in each other the beauty and mystery that is
so rare. Even in the weakest and most broken of us
there is miracle, there is the flow of life. It is easy to

forget this when we are on a bus, or running late, or having difficulty paying bills. It is hard to feel sacred when we feel ordinary, or to feel spiritual while lining up to buy an economy ticket for the train.

What can we do about life in our cities, how can we begin to turn around life styles that have no place for our real selves, where do we human beings find a more human way of living?

From an early age we may have been told we cannot and we should not, but we can and we should. Life is simply as it is. Benjamin Franklin said , 'Our limited perspective, our hopes and fears become our measure of life, and when circumstances do not fit our ideas, they become our difficulties.' We spend our lives wanting things. It is this very wanting that deceives us, that draws us in the opposite direction from joy; here in these distractions we find a void. This void can never be filled with material things, or healed by money, or even popularity or power.

There will always be critics, people to tell you what you are not able to do.

In a small town in the north of England one rainy day, I talked to the man sweeping the station platform. It was a dreary, drained and grey place. Factory chimneys scarred the dull horizon. Larry was overweight, rather sad looking and spoke slowly, and had been cleaning the railway station for twelve years. He had been married but was now divorced, and every year he went to the Egyptian galleries at the British Museum in London.

Since he was a child, Larry had been interested in Egypt. His voice changed, his eyes brightened and he spoke with animation and knowledge. When we stopped talking about ancient worlds, he once more became the dazed, disinterested old man pushing a balding broom, weary and bored. Larry's inspiration occupied a part of who he was, but had not moved further. Motivation is what happens when inspiration wakes us into being, leading us to action.

A friend of mine, Jimmie, a young Swedish artist, was struggling and felt defeated by life. Like a lot of young people in London, his energy was lured down cul-de-sacs of empty promises, misguided trust and 'transactional' or manipulative friendships. Jimmie had been taken advantage of time and again, and it was gnawing away at his self-esteem and self-worth.

Jimmie's small apartment had on the wall two very large canvases. The room was small and the paintings dimly lit and poorly hung. I looked at them, then at Jimmie. He was shy, embarrassed by them. He suggested we went to the kitchen and he talked about what film we might like to see that evening. Before me were two stunning nudes, painted with passion and abandon, intensity and compelling raw simplicity. Here was a man, not knowing what to do, where to find a job, how to move forward. He had a beautiful and powerful gift, but even when it hung before his eyes he did not see its worth.

It took a while to coax him to paint again. Even longer to convince him that it was something important. We bought paint and canvas together, and his talent awoke. He was not only inspired, but he was also motivated to the critical point of acting. His high fashion art and furniture sells in New York and Paris now, and has won awards.

Make 'some day' today, don't work towards your dreams, live them. Right now. There are people who tell you not to walk in the rain, or take a risk in a relationship. I remember people telling me why I should not go to Africa.

If we believe the ideas others put in our mind, we will spend our lives hiding, preparing, insuring ourselves and protecting the future. Larry found prudence like that safe, but the bars you live behind are made from the metal of self-doubt, fashioned by those in the cells of their own uncertainty. We can be like caged birds, wondering what our wings are for. 'Fear grows out of the things we think; it lives in our minds. Compassion grows out of the things we are, and lives in our hearts.' Barbara Garrison

Small children are told they can't play in the mud or run around the house naked; we teach children to be careful, and teachers are not allowed to hug children any more. We are told we cannot paint pictures

unless we stay on the paper, and we can't paint ourselves in yellow. As we grow older we are told that we
can't run around and that we are not aeroplanes or
birds, we can't sing or make noise and we are not
allowed to dance in class. Our culture is increasingly
regulatory and our actions prescribed and proscribed.
Look at how many signs you read every day telling
you what you cannot do.

Dreaming is allowing your imagination to talk to
you. It is not about being in contact with random
thoughts or passing fantasies but about imagining
things and believing in them. Many of us bury
dreams even before they have woken them within our
hearts. An old African man once told me, 'The trouble with a lot of people is they are afraid of what they
dream. Nothing more dangerous than a dream if you
are afraid of it, because then we stop feeling them
and then one day we can't feel our dreams any more.'

I said, 'And then?'

'Then people end up being who they are not.'

A traditional healer talked about corruption and violence in the big cities. We were talking about the rise
of greed and frustration. He told me the story of
Maidim. Maidim is a Maasai word meaning *I am not
able*. Maidim possesses the spirit of those who do not
see the sun, and if they stop seeing the light they
have their souls sucked from their faces so they do
not smile any more. Because they no longer live in

themselves but through others they never laugh any more and forget how to walk in the forest. When they are asked why they are sad though they have food and are healthy, they do not know. When they are told how to enjoy themselves all they can say is the name of the spirit that possesses them, Maidim!

Dreaming is allowing your imagination to talk to you.

The traps that we fall into are often the very goals that we set ourselves in the search for joy, and the ways in which we seek it. I meet many people who want to 'make a difference' and are frustrated. When you put down the book you are reading, reality takes over. There is rent to pay, travel cards and food to buy, bills are overdue, there is too little time to meet friends. Many people know what they need to do and what they want but they are not in a space that allows them to explore. Evidence that people want to better themselves lies in the success of self improvement books and courses. Since the publication of *All Will be Well*, I receive e-mails from people in every possible situation. That book was a reflection on how I have lived my own dream. Teresa, a single parent with children, wrote, 'That's great, but I need some idea of how that can help me where I am. I know by instinct I need to let myself out and give what I have to give.'

I now have over four thousand letters. No matter how humble your dream, how crazy your idea, believe in it, trust in it and draw friends to yourself who celebrate your passion. We all need dreams, the more mystical and amazing the better; never be afraid to live your dreams.

There will always be critics, people to tell you what you are not able to do. When I first went to Africa people said it was dangerous, you'll get sick, you have nothing to offer, you are wasting your time. It was Dr Joe Barnes, an old friend, who thought it was the obvious thing to do. 'Of course you should go. If you only help one single child, the child in front of you, go.' I have another friend called Tom. He has always been my best friend. I told him of my idea to create a different way of reaching poverty, not by seeing it as charity but something more radical. I am not sure whether Tom grasped my idea, I am not sure I did, but as always, he helped without me asking him for anything. Tom spent his holidays working hard and saving; he was careful with money and by the time he was twenty had saved thousands of pounds. Without blinking he gave it all to me to take to Africa, to see who we could help. Dr Joe and Tom believed in me and celebrated what had become our dream. Nearly thirty years later, with projects reaching many remote tribes, our work continues to grow. The weekly letters and continual support from Dr Joe allowed our work to flourish.

Billy, a retired UN peace keeper from Canada visited our Maasai projects in the 90s. Billy was a simple man, in poor health but with a massive heart. He saw the children in their classroom in the semi-desert. The classroom was barely four walls of rusty corrugated iron, with no windows or doors. The children had no books and sat on the earth. They wrote with little twigs on their thighs. He visited a clinic where the nurse had no medicines and saw crippled children who had never moved from their homes as they had never had a wheelchair. Billy met me briefly as he headed back to Nairobi. His eyes were full of tears and his hands trembled. 'I am not going to say much, because I bet you heard it all before, but I tell you, I'll be back, watch this space...' Billy went back to Canada and started sharing his dream with

We suck, crawl and stagger; we fall only to get-up again

friends. He was a peace keeper and knew a vast network of veterans. He started going to hospitals and asking for wheelchairs. One hospital told him they could not help. Every morning he would turn up at the administrator's office and sit outside and keep asking. He got his wheelchair. His dream was to do whatever he could with what he had and he started sending medical supplies. When he ran out of money, he sold his rare Chinese coins, then he sold his hunting guns. In time he sent more and more hospital equipment. Billy was trying hard to find as many ways as he could to reach the people he wanted to help. It was not about development strategy, it was not about big issues, it was just about a personal response to what he saw. At first glance Billy looks like an overweight, tired, old man in bad health. It is only when you get up close to him that you see the boundless energy, the passionate delight in his embrace, the pleasure he has in being with you. Billy now sends containers of medical supplies to South America, Asia and across Africa.

Everyone said he couldn't, some told him he should not try, others told him to rest. Many people encouraged him to send a donation or take out a standing order, but that was not Billy's dream.

IRENEUS – A JOURNEY *part II* ▬▬▬▬▬▬▬▬▬

Ireneus had left the city though his friends told him not to go beyond the horizon and not to venture to the strange lands beyond the walls built by their fathers. He climbed for days towards the mountain of dreams, he was in search of Saralunar the mystic. Each night he would have the same dream, a wonderful dream. In the dream Ireneus was as a being filled with light. His eyes could see into the purer heart of things and his soul was one with everything that lived. In the dream Ireneus had a gift, that unto whomever he came he brought a great power. Into the hearts of those he met he could pour light from his touch, and this light could cast away their fears, take away their burdens and remove their sickness. Ireneus did not understand the dream, so he sought Saralunar. He walked through the valley of sorrow and past the marshes of despair and through the forest where the sirens lived. Many before him had tried to pass through the forest, but they became seduced by the beauty that lived there and never left the glades of the forest, forever ensnared by the magic there. They believe that the hidden world is an illusion and that dreams are for children.

Those about him told him not to leave. His lover shared her nightmares and his father bade him wait as his mother cried, for they had many fears. Ireneus grew uncertain and his friends prepared a banquet.

He turned as he had before, to put down his bag and go with them. As he turned he heard the soft whisper of the old woman who was watching from the garden. Leto beckoned him. His grandmother was very old, these days moving slowly, yet her face shone more radiantly than all the others. What you do now will be in your tomorrow, my child, your fate is in this choice, listen to your heart, not to fears. She drew him to her and she spoke softly to his heart, and his eyes welled up, and he kissed her softly. As he left the gates of the city, he carried in him her words, 'They have forgotten how to sail their ships which are tied up in the harbour never to sail, they want you to moor yours beside them. Do what is within you, never what is in everyone else, my child.'

Ask yourself:
Do fears restrict my dreams?

What did I do today that takes me closer to my dream?

When will I achieve my dream?

In the next few days, solve a number puzzle like SuDoku. If you already do number puzzles, try a harder one than usual.

Some topics for meditation:
What is the greatest obstacle to the life you want to live? Meditate on life without that obstacle.

Am I living my dreams?

The self and others

*A human being is part of a whole,
called by us the 'Universe'*

Albert Einstein

When we are born, everything is new,
everything is wondrous and possible, and the world revolves around
us. As we grow, we learn at a staggering rate; our bodies learn to snuggle, hug and
touch. With encouragement and praise we learn and
thrive surrounded by love and affection. We suck,
crawl and stagger; we fall only to get-up again but
this we do surrounded by gentleness and trust,
acceptance and delight. Before we ever utter a word
we form our primal reference points. It is from these
primal experiences that we establish the core of who
we think we are.

Our parents unconsciously programme us through
their behaviour, voices, tone and tenderness. As we
begin to be conscious of ourselves as independent
entities, we evolve responses and reactions to the
world outside ourselves. We decide when we will

laugh, when we will cry, when we will giggle. This is the starting point and the gate we pass through into self-knowledge. The insight into my own 'self' is the first step of wisdom. It is here that we discover self-love.

Selfhood is about identity. Our state of being, our 'self-state', need not be set by what is in our heads or influenced by what is going on in our environment. We can anchor ourselves in the truth of who we are, and become resilient to daily frustrations or be influenced by the moods of others. We can use the following assertions as stepping stones, as constants in our changing world:

Ask yourself:
What can I do tomorrow to take me closer to my dream?

When will I achieve my dream?

Some topics for meditation:
I am created by love, and made to love

Each breath is an act of creation

I am power

Self-loving versus self-centred

Self-love is the opposite of self-centredness. When we are self-centred, we are pre-occupied with our whims, satisfying our desires, conversations about us; we are the priority with regard to agenda and expectations. On the other hand self-love has no introspections. It is 'other' focused because it is a celebration. It is the realisation of goodness and energy within us. It delights in the presence of the 'self' and by nature delights in others. Self-love gives without thought because the self is full of positive energy and thought. Hatred and anger are always impotent. They diminish us.

A man I know moves from one worry to the next like stepping stones. His negative thinking has such control over his life that he is locked in a pattern of self-rejection. Steve is constantly in conflict because he is hypersensitive about what other people say. If they say something nice he thinks they are lying and if they ignore him he thinks they hate him. Steve is demanding because he

> *The most powerful force in our lives is the power we have over our own thoughts.*

needs the acceptance of others and external affirmation. If Steve loved himself, he would not demand from others. Internal acceptance would be enough, self-completion and self-becoming is not reliant on the outside.

We rarely think of ourselves as self-centred, but sometimes we view the world through such a narrow telescope that we can miss the feelings and needs around us. We can fail to see the journeys of those we love, and be oblivious to their silences and signs.

THE PRINCE'S BRIDE

A young prince was once travelling through his country and found in a distant village the most perfect girl he had ever seen. She was the incarnation of beauty, pure and in every way divine to him, so he worshipped her. He robed her in silks and gold, showered her with every gift possible and the whole village rejoiced. He bestowed land and titles on her family and gave them wealth. He brought the beautiful girl to his palace in the great city by the sea and there he surrounded her with every opulence and treasure. He planned to marry her and the king was amazed at her angelic beauty, the queen smiled for she had never had a daughter. The young prince was blinded utterly by his love and he had never felt such peace or joy in his life. This gift from heaven was all he had ever dreamed of and he was gentle and tender to her, respectful and gracious in every way. His paradise was the very thought of her and he trembled in his every thought of her. Every time he gazed upon her, he was complete and tears of joy filled his eyes upon the mention of her name.

As the weeks passed and the wedding approached the beautiful girl became ill. After days of examination by the greatest physicians and wise men, the prince was told that she was slowly dying. The prince was bereft and nothing could console him. The oldest of the wise told him that there might be one who knew a cure and he lived in the forest on the great mountains that were covered with snow. At once riders were sent to bring the healer to the palace and all the time the girl grew worse.

After a few days the hermit of the forest, a friend of Saralunar, came to the prince in the golden hall of the palace by the sea. He held the manicured jewelled hands of the handsome prince in his and closed his eyes bowing his head. The prince spoke not, for he was afraid and a silence passed within him in the presence of the old man. There was light within his gentle eyes and the invisible was strong about him, the power of the unknown was visible, so people fell still near him.

The hermit raised his eyes still whispering, as if in conversation, then he spoke. He told the prince that he could heal the girl and restore her to full life and that she could be completely happy and know limitless joy. The prince smiled, and then the hermit said that this could only be done with a medicine that was very bitter and that the treatment cost a great deal. 'Any cost... No cost is too great!' replied the young prince. 'My Son,' replied the hermit, gentleness in his soft voice, 'the medicine will be painful for you not for the girl.' The prince stepped back, and the king and queen took each other's hands. 'In your love, you see the shrine of your beloved at which you worship, not knowing that with your adoration you are burying her. The girl you adore is the dream in your imagining, this child dying possesses her own dreams that lie in her tomb and she would rather join them then abandon them.' The prince fell on his knees, 'but you said she could be happy and healed.' 'Yes, but not with you my child, she is in love with a simple shepherd in her village who is her joy and her dream… let her go!' 'I never knew,' whispered the prince through long deep breaths. The hermit continued, 'you had found the fulfilment of your own dream and fell in love with your heart's desire, and in the flood of joy that followed, you did not hear her soft whispers or see the tears in her eyes.' The prince looked up at the old man, then over to his parents and bowed his head. He loved her so much, how could he let her go? The old man had left the great golden doors and passed into the streets even as the saddened parents embraced their shattered son. He loved her beyond all else, could he let her go?

We only have the power to let go if we really love what is within us, because then there is no need for others to fill our void, to meet our illusions or needs. This is a fable about each of us. So often in the course of our lives we are in moments when the most loving thing to do is let go, no matter what the cost.

Ask yourself:
Do I plan quality time with myself, for myself?

What are my worries?

How can I shorten the list of worries by planning?

Self-possession versus self pre-occupation

The most powerful force in our lives is the power we have over our own thoughts. We can choose how we will react to people, how we will behave and when to let go of a habit. We can choose how we will speak, the words we use, the things we will do and the places where we will be. When our beliefs about ourselves are full of doubt, we see a flawed 'self' but when we believe in ourselves then we shine from within, and it shows.

Taking control of our thoughts is only possible when we are not distracted by the 'stuff,' the maintenance and survival that drown out the things that matter. When we are unhappy or confused, we feel vulnerable and become so preoccupied with ourselves that we fail to see the big picture. Being absorbed in ourselves creates introspection and negative patterns of behaviour and stress. If our mind is calm and we are comfortable within ourselves, we are in harmony with what is happening around us and have a sense of emotional balance. When our mind is still and our body relaxed we are self-possessed. We need to train ourselves to think and act differently. Each moment we have is a pure gift – it is just there, not earned by any of us, so precious – even the richest and most powerful cannot buy more time on this earth. The secret is to celebrate the miracle of each moment as best as we can.

We need to discover the power, the present, and the mystery of living the now with YES. This celebration is self-possession. This self-realisation is about delighting in ourselves, enjoying the gift of ourselves and laughing at ourselves.

Often we are so tied to the past and anxious of what the future brings that we may miss the possibilities and chances that present themselves to us. In tribal Africa, our notion of time is a perception; it is simply an idea. I remember asking an old Maasai man about time – he laughed and told me that a lot of white people were very afraid of time because they never enjoyed being with it, they never grew to live in time. Instead they counted it and tried to catch up with it. He was saying that life itself is in the breath of this moment, now, and not in all the breath we have ever taken before – life might be in a breath or in two seconds but who knows, our life forms now – only now. The old Maasai man also said that time

Freeing ourselves from our addictions and traps, we can create the life we really want.

was 'big... very, very big' but that it had an end – and that was when I smiled and thought of another way of being.

Wonder, delight and love fill our moments with grace and memory. Life is about celebrating the here and now, living these moments and finding grace every time we wake up. It is our choice how we see our now. The practice of presence is to feel the energy of creation, to taste the miracles of life here, as it is right now. Another person can experience the same tragedies or joys as we do, but react and feel completely differently about it. A fundamental part of making this work is letting go of everything negative, of everything limiting. We become more successful than we ever dreamed of and see the world truly through different eyes, a world full of wonder.

We need to feel the power and energy of life within us, rather than be limited by what we have been trained to think.

An open mind makes it possible for us to be objective and be aware of alternative possibilities when trying to understand ourselves. A young man, Matt, talked about his future. Matt had a history of let downs, health problems, financial and relationship disasters. He had moved from job to job, often from one group of friends to another. Matt had trapped himself in his own web of conditioned responses and cyclic reactions. As he shared his story it became apparent what was wrong. He was carrying on his back all the failure and pain of every mistake he had ever made. In each relationship he was waiting to be rejected, and if it did not happen he would trigger a set of events to create a rejection.

He was tormented by problems and consumed by self-doubt. When solutions were suggested he had a flurry of reasons why he could not eat well or why he could not make changes in his life to improve his situation. Matt was unable and unwilling to consider the possibility that the cycles of negative experience were generated by the way in which he chose to react. It was only when Matt began to see the triggers of his stress and the default responses he used that he began to change.

He learned coping techniques to calm his mind. Soon Matt began to control his anger, he began to sleep better without waking up anxious and worried, and he learned not to be afraid. Such changes do not happen overnight. It takes years of thinking in loops to create patterns that determine how we model ourselves. It takes time to unlearn negative cycles, to create positive healing thoughts and behaviour.

Finding a purpose gives direction to our efforts. Self-knowledge can be pursued in many ways, each leading potentially to greater harmony; be it through meditation, self-reflection, stillness, keeping a journal or challenging ourselves. I have always found it helpful to spend time every day emptying my mind of everything negative, any stray thought and any source of anxiety. I take each fragmented imagining, any unwelcome word, every reason of worry and I reflect on it. I see it for what it is - nothing. I take the totality of these concerns and doubts, fears and energies and cast them from me. I do this too with my body, also taking any tension, stress or pain and removing it completely. There are many ways of doing this, through contemplation, meditation or Yoga, attaining self-awareness and inner stillness.

Ask yourself:
Who controls my fears?

Am I gentle with myself?

Which of my gifts have I taken pleasure in this week?

Have a pencil and paper, and do this quickly - quickly enough not to think about it: think of something you want. Now quickly draw it.

Some topics for meditation:
I am the source of my own feelings.

Others do not make me happy or sad, I choose my own reactions.

power of others

✵ ✵ ✵ ✵ ✵ ✵ ✵

We are all energy, within us is the power to illuminate or diminish each other. Everyone outside our inner self is 'other.' Others of course have many dimensions and manifestations. There are the six billion humans who live across the planet usually referred to as 'they' often alien, rarely relevant to where we live or what we do. There are those who live in our world or influence us from a distance, they might be the politicians, actors or musicians who influence our culture and media, advertising or reality television - the background noise and iconography of our cultural moment.

At a local level there are the others who are in our physical realm, people we see or with whom we transact. They might be people we see regularly, classmates, teachers and colleagues. They are present but they rarely rock our world. Closer still, are those who are woven into the fabric of our lives. These people often determine us, move within our thoughts and imaginings, they are rooted in who we are, they are family, friends who matter, those whose lives are part of us. If we are lucky, somewhere in there will be

114

a few who know us from within, who accept us despite utterly seeing us, cherish us just as we are.

Here is an experiment you might want to try. I recently made a mind map of everyone I knew. It was not of people who had influenced my thinking; they were on a different fresco. In the centre of the page I drew a circle and I called it *JOY*. From it I drew different arteries. In the different places and areas of my life I wrote down the names of everyone I knew. I divided them by country and by relationship, by level of intimacy and by the joy of my relationship to them. In my mind-map there were energy currents of people who were wonderfully supportive and dynamic; there were those I worked with, and others I knew socially. As the map grew, I taped on more pages. I ended up with arteries, veins, capillaries, all connecting a huge number of names. There were people who were on the outskirts of my world, others who touched me deeply, and some who hurt me and others who misunder-stood me.

On this paper was an iconographic map of my life of people's presence as energy. At its centre was the

We all need to make space and real time for those who help us become who we are.

thickest artery of all, it shot straight into the circle of JOY. The names of five people were written on that artery. Of the hundreds in my world, the dozens I work with, the many who are friends, there were five who were at the centre. These people do not see the public image, they see beyond the visible and accept and embrace me without limitation or condition. Throughout my life these closest to me cherish my inner being. It is this energy that illuminates and restores us, floods into our life when the rest of the world walks away.

From time to time it is good to prioritise and remember who these people are. They are so much a part of us that sometimes we take them for granted. We know they are always there for us and sometimes we can forget to celebrate them.

We receive so much energy from being with them. If you make your own inner light map of those who fill your heart, you will see the names of those who lift you simply by knowing you. I called each of the five and reminded them how essential and wonderful they were and how much they enriched my humanity by being in my life.

One of the five people in the centre of my mind-map was Joe. His simple grace and humour floods the most cynical person with kindness. Joe actually never needs to say anything to inspire you, he just does it. When we began our work in Africa nearly three decades ago, we faced impossible odds. Whenever I told Joe of the scale of poverty and need, he placed his palm on my trembling hand (I was all gusto and zeal). 'Mike, don't worry about "impossible", just do everything possible, just do the best you possibly can, with whatever you have for the child in front of you... one at a time, you don't need to do it all, just start with the child looking at you, wherever you are.'

Through Dr Joe Barnes I met Ronán.

I was in the northern deserts in the middle of a famine; we were fighting the diarrhoea which kills so many children in the Sub-Sahara. I called one of those five people whose profound gentleness and love touch my life. I have known people of many denominations who regularly pray in their sanctuaries; I have yet to meet one with as much selfless humanity and compassion as this man. Ronán Conroy answered the phone in Ireland; I asked about his young son,

No one you will meet has ever received too much kindness, we all need more.

Michael who is very special and very gentle. Michael had the flu. I started to ask Ronán about ways to measure the care of the terminally ill, as he has great ways to help the dying.

Ronán was having none of it. He heard the tiredness in my voice, he knows me, and he was more interested in my own well-being. Ronán has always read me better than I could read myself and he not only always knows what to say, but also what to do. Like all special friends, just connecting regenerates you in ways no sleep can.

Often we use words loosely. We throw words like 'love' around, depreciating their meaning.

There are people we meet casually on occasion. We hang out with them sometimes and go for lunch. Some people pass through our lives and we barely remember their second name. Others, closer to us; we might study together, share interests or watch sports. Their children might go to the same school as ours, we might meet for dinner. We exchange greeting cards for festivals or birthdays. Then there are those who matter to us. We have known them and their families for years, shared holidays with them, been in each other's homes, laughed together, shared problems, confided in and supported one another. Within this group there is also the *freond*. The old English *freond* is the etymon of the word friend 'to love deeply.'

> *The soul should always stand ajar,*
> *ready to welcome the ecstatic*
> *experience.*

> Emily Dickinson

A freond is rare and is the one who embraces all that is our being, our darkness and our light, our weakness and frailty as well as our magic. The freond is the one who accepts our contradictions and enigmas, celebrates us as we are without judgement. These energies double our joy and halve our grief. A freond is so tuned into our hearts that we do not need to be with each other to be united, there is a powerful current between the *freond* and

It is important to have people close to us who respect and value us, those who will cherish and support, nurture and heal us.

us. We all need to make space and real time for those who help us become who we are.

The place to begin is to always welcome the stranger into your life. Everyone deserves to drink from your pool, all creation can be celebrated through you and be the richer for having met you. Treat everyone you meet as if you may never see them again.

Try to scatter your life with acts and deeds of small greatness, moments of warmth and kindness. These are the stars in your universe, and the wonder of your life. Everyone you meet presents an opportunity to be surprised by joy; each stranger is a possible friend. No one you will meet has ever received too much kindness, we all need more. The secret of happiness is to give of your heart.

NLP explores self-conditioning, unlearning, power and positive rethinking and reprogramming. Reprogramming ourselves to become empowered is nothing new. The techniques have been around for thousands of years in martial art disciplines, meditation, self healing and other ancient traditions. Today, NLP is widely used in therapy, rehabilitation, treatment of depression and stress. It is used in business to improve management, sales and inter-personal skills; in education, to understand learning styles better, develop rapport with students and parents and to aid motivation. It simply allows you to change, adopt or eliminate behaviours, habits and patterns of action. It gives you the ability to choose your mental, emotional, and physical states of well-being.

We need to feel the power and energy of life within us, rather than be limited by what we have been trained to think. We need to be able to create the energies and emotions we want rather than be manipulated by stress and the pressures around us. We need to escape the limitations of linear time and explore dynamic time through which we create ourselves. To do this means taking responsibility for our own life, never giving in to feeling overwhelmed or defeated.

We can transform little conflicts into little joys, small flash points of tension into experiences of calm.

We can change our experience of time, utterly and permanently. Freeing ourselves from our addictions and traps, we can create the life we really want. That is what NLP offers, as meditation and contemplation also do. There are many routes, but the transforming power is not NLP. The secret of time and the power of releasing ourselves is to become compassionate in the present, right now. Like a magnifying glass we can draw together our power to create love, and love in this moment. It is through this act that we become fully human, fully alive. It is in this act that we become wonder.

We have reflected on the power of others who can touch, heal and uplift us, but the world is not only full of gentle people who celebrate us. There are people we meet on the battlefield of life who can drain, manipulate and diminish us. A friend of mine recently told me that when he was a young kid at school he had nightmares and would feel sick about going to school each morning. He was dyslexic, but was considered lazy. One day a teacher brought him up to the front of the class. He was so tiny he could not reach the black board, and the teacher lifted him up so he could write on the board, '*I AM STUPID.*' The trauma has been such that he still has nightmares and when he passes the school now, he cannot turn his eyes towards the buildings.

A woman I knew stayed in an abusive relationship for ten years. Then as many do, she went from that destructive relationship into another. Each time her boyfriend hurt her, he would apologise and be affectionate. Until the next time. The only way out of the downward spiral of a destructive relationship is to leave, and leave completely. These power relationships feed off intimidation, dependency, fear and self loathing. The patterns are always the same and the cycles are tragically predictable. Increasingly frequent cycles of argument and anger build up tension. Incidents range from emotional to physical loss of control. Shame, rage, guilt, terror, futility and desperation scar the emotional landscape. And then there is the making up. The making up often involves tenderness, mutual forgiveness, denial and excuse from both. Then it happens again. While all relationships have their ups and downs, it is important to realise when we are stuck in a rut.

An influential man, many years ago, was in a position to help a group of us setting up a medical programme. He was an angry, impatient person. In his words was tension, ordinary questions were clipped, loud demands

> *We do not need to understand everything to delight in it.*

rather than being calm and objective. Some fifteen minutes into the meeting he stabbed a finger in my direction and told me to explain our proposal. I smiled and rose to stand. I apologised for taking his time and told him that even though I knew he could help us, we did not actually need his help. I told him that the only way he could raise his voice was if he was permitted to do so. My colleagues were out the door before I was, but before I left I said that I have no place in my world for anger. This had never happened to him before.

Whether in college or at home, at work or in our

social lives, we are sometimes in situations where we are exposed and vulnerable. It is important that we have people close to us who respect and value us, those who will cherish and support, nurture and heal us.

The power of the 'other' can transform our lives forever; we need to make sure that it is the friends and the healers, the freonds and those that love us, who transform it.

Ask yourself:
Do I bring joy?

Do I feel accepted?

Do I feel valued?

What can strengthen my sense of self tomorrow?

How does happiness fit into my goals?

Choose some music – try reaching for something unfamiliar.

Some topics for meditation:
The qualities I offer as a friend.

The qualities my closest friend offers me.

Wonder and becoming, the magic within

Being still, just still enough, and long enough, to see the perfection in front of our eyes

Within us is the seed of creation and the freedom to love in the present; in this gift lies all 'other,' our ability to transform everything that is forever. It is becoming wonder and being light. We do not spend enough of our day in the mystery of the gifts we are given. So many people at the end of their lives express regret. They speak of the things they left undone, the places they would have visited, the times they worked too much, played too little. It may be too late when we realise that what is really valuable, what gives us meaning, gets ignored while we are caught up in trivia. We have reflected on the way we live and the way we are, how habits can block energy. In our growing awareness of self, of others and the insights that awaken new choices, there is one underlying purpose. It is to rejoice and celebrate in the wonder of life and

You cannot lose another life than the one you are living now.

become the happiness we were born to be. It is about being touched by grace and amazed, not bored by life. It is seeing the countless miracles all around us and the unfolding of power within us. It is realising that we are miracle, we are magical; we are wonder.

Of course we exist in the real world, the world of impatience and deadlines, moods and pressures. There are bills to pay and problems to sort out, and there are times when everything goes wrong. This was already true in the second century when the emperor Marcus Aurelius said in his second book of *Meditations*, 'When you wake up in the morning, tell yourself: The people I deal with today will be meddling, ungrateful, arrogant, dishonest, jealous and surly.' Sometimes people can be mean. This is no less true in the modern world, when an immigration official might be deliberately rude just because he can be, a traffic policeman might be aggressive and unreasonable, and in our daily lives when a friend might be upsetting or a child might say something truly hurtful.

People can express feeling drained, in pain or angry in many different ways. Sometimes we might not even realise that we are being negative. Energy masked as humour can be a whip we use on those nearby. We can all be hurtful, all be unkind. We can return an angry retort, or we can choose to create something else. We can transform little conflicts into little joys, small flash points of tension into experiences of calm. Someone who is having a bad day may generate more anger around them by being rude or impatient. Met with gentleness, that little sunshine might help them feel better.

Whenever there is a flame, no matter how tiny, it can grow.

I remember an obnoxious waitress in a small café on a rainy Monday morning in Toronto. She could not have been more unhelpful. When I paid the bill, she threw the change on the table. As I left I put a $20 bill near the till, smiled at her, and said that I hoped her day would brighten up. For the first time she actually looked at me, and then she allowed herself a little smile. None of us know the burdens the other may be carrying, or the pain that is in their heart. It matters a lot every time we say something positive, give a compliment, give our time and listen to each other.

What has this to do with wonder? Everything. If wonder is being awoken and surprised, delighted and touched, then this is how we bring wonder into our lives. By sharing amazement in the tiny things. In a gesture, a smile or just in recognition. Wonder is something else as well. It is the state of gratitude and child-like amazement at everything because everything is simply, truly, amazing. It is to ask ourselves, the whole of ourselves, to rejoice in it all. It is about experiencing and tasting, not analysing or describing. We do not need to understand everything to delight in it. We need to be able to accept mystery, to embrace uncertainty, and to realise that in the end the great design and the harmony of it all will be fine. It is this unfolding that is the fabulous adventure of life.

> *There are only two ways to live
> your life. One as though nothing is
> a miracle.*
>
> *The other is as though everything is
> a miracle.*

Albert Einstein

I remember breaking down in the African bush with Tom Hogan. We were 50 miles away from the nearest town, it was late and the old car just died. Tom looked at the engine and said, 'Well I've good news and I've better news, which would you like first?' I said, 'Great, you can fix it?' 'There's nothing wrong with the engine, the car's grand.' 'That's great Tom,' I said, 'let's go!' 'Ah yea, well a drop of petrol would help and we can get that in the morning, no bother.'

After I had resigned myself to our position, I then enquired what the good news was and the better news. 'The good news is that there's nothing wrong at all, and the better news is that we get to camp out and look at what we have.' I followed his gaze and there before me it was. In the pitch black of the night was a vast firmament, galaxies of stars exploding across the African Savannah as far as the eye could see. There before us was the hand of God on such a scale, in the stillness of divine presence. It was a moment that touched into the deepest cord of my being. Into what 'being' meant, and why we were here in this perfect creation. There were legions upon legions of stars. I stopped thinking and those experiences, deeper than reason, had flooded over me.

We are the authors of our own next chapter, and we can be whatever we choose

We so often lose the gifts of creation along the way because we are too busy going somewhere else. In Zen one is taught to stop all the frenetic activity, stop the moving, going, learning, training and working. Stop. When we stop we have time to experience not just the 'everything,' but in that 'everything' we experience our oneness with the breath of the universe. In this we become utterly conscious of the things that give us most pleasure and make us belong.

You will see how little you need to do to live an exciting life. Stuff gets in the way and drains our energy. All the stuff we have will vanish, be thrown out or passed on, yet we spend so much of our energy, and even our self-worth in accumulating things. The culture of celebrity insists that we constantly re-examine ourselves in the mirror, comparing ourselves to an airbrushed ideal.

You cannot lose another life than the one you are living now, or live another one than the one you are losing; so unless we rejoice in the life that is ours, and go for it completely, we will waste the gift. The span we live is small, as small as the corner of the earth in which we live it. It is over in the blink of an eye, yet we waste the incredible awesome gift of it.

How many people do you know who are not delighted or excited by what they do but they do it anyway. Run through the list of those you knew who worked in vain, who failed to do what they should have or could have. We need to go from one selfless act to another, then to another, and programme ourselves to be that way instinctively. To be gentle, polite, generous, caring and joyful. This is the most primal NLP, and it really works, try it. It's the most liberating thing you will ever do.

Think how much is going on inside you every second – in your soul, in your body. Why should it astonish you that so much more – everything that happens in that all-embracing unity, the world is happening at the same time?

As we become conscious of the mystery, and aware that everything is a gift, we can start to re-examine how we understand ourselves, how we relate to the rest of creation and where we are in the vastness of the universe. We need to grasp that whatever happens has always happened, and always will. We will understand where to channel our energy and action when we reflect within ourselves and decide. What is it that I want? To keep on breathing? To achieve certain goals? To create this home? To act according to my deepest self I need to realise my true self and free it. This is awakening to the wonder and the limitless power I have over my future.

External events are the wild card and always change the goalposts, the reality of situations and problems, little disasters or blessings outside our control constantly hit us from the first conversation we have to the last text message of the day. Our actions and everything that happens today rely on how we see these things in relation to the universe, where we see ourselves in the vastness of creation. No pessimist ever discovered the secret of the stars, or sailed to an uncharted land, or opened a new doorway for the human spirit.

Each morning on the dust track in the African bush, on the way to the feeding stations, I saw two old women, Turkana grandmothers, living in the harsh deserts, collecting shrubs. They flattened the dry twigs in the sand and wove them into a tiny hut. They spent weeks doing it. They were old and fragile and tried hard in the hot sun. I would sometimes stop to leave them supplies, and once left them a goat for milk. They were always smiling.

We do not find happiness, we create it.

One day I passed and saw their little hut smashed into bits and scattered across the scorched earth. Elephants had passed by and walked through their little patch. Laughing and joking they started to build their little home again. These two old sisters were the last that remained of their family, the rest had died one by one in the drought. They were bare-foot and their possessions were a cooking pan and a tin cup. They rebuilt their little house and, being frail and delicate, it blew apart in a sand storm. Each time I visited, they had a cup of warm dirty water to share and laughter came from somewhere inside them, joy dancing behind their sparkling eyes. We gave them a tough army tent to live in, but it was stolen the next week. I suggested they move to a safer area, but they had known these lands all their lives and were happy where they were.

In the days that followed, the famine eased and each time we passed by the two old sisters, we left poles and wire and wood. Soon another little hut was built. An old man, unable to walk farther came and they helped him to build a tiny hut beside their own. A young mother came and she too was welcomed and lived beside the old women. The last time I visited, there was a thriving village around the dry patch of earth.

Whenever there is a flame, no matter how tiny, it can grow. Where there is a message of goodness it will endure. Sometimes we can feel like our little hut is falling to bits, sometimes it gets crushed by passing elephants. Sometimes our work gets blown away. And sometimes what we have built is something that will endure.

> *He who knows enough is enough*
> *will always have enough.*

> Lao -Tzu

The wonder I am talking about is not like walking along a moonlit beach elated by the moment or stuck by beauty. This wonder is a state of being, a disposition through which we can live at a deeper level, amazed and enriched by everything even by loss, pain and suffering. Wonder is about waking up amazed.

Today. It is about seeing how the ordinary things can elate and excite us, inspire us with gratitude and awe.

Wonder is like love, the more we give to others, the more we have. It electrifies everything we sense, magnifies experience and generates insatiable curiosity. It is passionate and instils delight, opening the door of the mind. We can find this wonder by shedding stale thinking, and seeing the overwhelming mystery around us. In this creative freedom we give ourselves the power to become.

Ask yourself:
Do I anticipate something negative in my future?

How can I transform it, just by changing the way I view it?

What last surprised me?

When can I next see the moon?

Some topics for meditation:
What wonder did I see this week?

What is 'enough'?

The secret of becoming

Happiness is our natural condition

Changing ourselves is about changing the way in which we relate to others, changing our relationships starts with how we love ourselves and that depends on our power to listen within. Listening is a very deep art of giving, and giving is the way in which we find ourselves. When we learn to understand the child within, we need to practise the rare art of forgiveness because only in forgiving can we find delight. The only thing within us is the love we have given away. Happiness pours out of giving into every part of our awareness.

There is a simple way in which our lives can find new meaning and wonder; it is so simple that very few people ever actually live it. The secret of staying in love, the path to being fully alive lies in the way of joy. Every time we are touched, every time we laugh or cry, we do so because we are reminded of who and what we are supposed to be. Life begins full of delight, wonder and awe.

We are born to celebrate, and that means seeing not only the magic and wonder around us but the funny, delicious humour that pervades each day. We need to unlearn everything we have assumed or been taught, question ourselves, and jump into life with faith and passion in the little things and soon we will be able to be passionate in everything.

> *Put your heart, mind, intellect and soul even to your smallest acts. This is the secret of success.*
>
> Swami Sivananda

We are the authors of our own next chapter, and we can be whatever we choose, we can decide to be happy. Much of our time is taken up dealing with different types of stuff, and a lot of that stuff is about fear. Once we let go of fear during our day, we start to see amazing things happening all around us.

Inner calm grows out of being completely here, in the moment of 'now.' This book is about the now; it is about the tasting of

What is life? Only a procession of moments. When we take possession of our moments, we can choose how we live.

joy that is within us. It is a change that will transform our bodies, and it starts with attitude, with breaking habits, with the way we choose to see. This perception is the dawn of owning ourselves; it is freeing our waking thoughts to perceive the centre. By practising daily to change our perception and action, choosing thoughts and behaviour consciously, we radically can alter our mind flow.

Joy is not something that happens to us, but something we make inside us, and can then share with others. We do not find happiness, we create it. So too with love, we do not really fall in love or give love, we become love. As with all becoming, all great adventures, they are made up of single steps, single movements.

The secret of joy is the secret of love. It is the compassionate listening within that creates balance and wonder. This breathes light into all our thinking, the smallest acts become dynamic, the simplest conversations have new meaning. It is the path of seeing what is worth celebrating in the gift of now, realising it will never come again. It is here now, within us, and it will surprise us, awaken us and change our world forever. Our faith is our daily life, it's what drives our words, thoughts and deeds.

Ask yourself:
What is the next chapter of my life, as I write it now?

What can I celebrate tomorrow?

Could I try wearing a different style of clothes tomorrow?

Some topics for meditation:
What am I becoming?

What is my dream?

Presence

Take possession of the moment, and from being a
spectator in your life, become the author

I t is time to change the world around us. It is
time to set fire to the hearts around us, it is
time to take the initiative and repair our
world. In every way and in any way, now is the
moment in our lives that we can change the world
forever. We have the power to change tomorrow by
simply organising our present lives in a new way. It is
how we reconstruct the now - how we approach what
is in front of us that will bring about the change.

We need to understand that we are already miracle,
we already have power within us to heal and to make
whole. We are able to give and to forgive in a way
that will transform ourselves and everyone around
us. In every person I meet, is an opportunity to
encourage and support. Today I may meet a shop

assistant in a supermarket, a woman waiting in the rain for a bus, an impatient driver stressed out behind me hooting his horn. There are so many chances I will have to be more patient, more gentle, more positive, more engaged in the lives of those I meet. The society we live in today creates its own anxieties in a frantic rush just to keep up with ourselves. We can de-stress by beginning to make decisions of how we will choose to respond to this moment. We can decide that here, to the person before me, I will give my energy, my attention, my presence. I can choose to smile, choose to listen, act with grace and patience. These are the choices that change our attitudes and our conditioned behaviour gradually shifts towards something new.

For many of us, happiness is a memory or an aspiration. It is something we recall and desire to experience again. Everything we remember exists in our minds as time – it is really as simple as a smile, a kiss, and a sunset. In other words, we remember moments, because what is life? Only a procession of moments. When we take possession of our moments, we can choose how we live. We remember most deeply our emotions, not our thoughts, we recall our feelings not our beliefs. Beliefs do not make us happy – but how we live them might.

In the 16th century a Carmelite brother wrote a short book called, *The Practice of the Presence of God.* In it, Brother Lawrence said that if we realise that this moment can never be repeated, can never be relived

– we see it in a very different way. There will never be another now, this the only time you can ever taste or know; this now.

We live in a world where many people are dislocated from the moment they are in. They are not living in the moment; they are rushing through it from somewhere or to something. There is no way to happiness. Happiness is not a state of being, happiness is our power now by becoming in the present. There is an African saying, 'you are how you live, and you become what you do.'

We need to celebrate this in every situation we experience. To paraphrase Ecclesiastes; to every thing in us there is a season, and a time to every purpose. A time to let go, a time to cling on, a time to be born, and a time to die; a time to plant, and a time to pluck up that which is planted; a time to break down, and a time to build up; a time to weep, and a time to laugh; a time to mourn, and a time to dance; a time to say hello, and a time to say goodbye; a time to embrace, and a time to refrain from embracing; a time to get, and a time to lose; a time to keep, and a time to cast away; a time to be alone and a time to be with others; a time to be silent, and a time to speak; a time to love, and a time to let go; a time of chaos, and a time of peace.

If that is so, we might ask ourselves, 'Is my life consistent with what I say I believe in?' 'Do my deeds match my values?' Presence requires attention, attention requires listening. Listening is a deeply spiritual practice and the most essential path to awareness, awareness is the gateway to awakening and awakening is the dawn of all joy.

Listening takes energy because you are giving the other person part of your life force by focusing your attention on them. It is difficult to be attentive to another person until we are attentive to ourselves, and this is why we need to listen to ourselves and create time for that listening. Mother Teresa once said, 'We cannot do great things on this earth. We can only do little things with great love.'

All we really have to do is to focus on those little acts of kindness, things we can do, right now.

The root of frustration is our unwillingness to accept life as being different from our expectations. Most of the time we should choose kindness over being right. If we want to change the 'me' here and now, we need to become fully involved in every detail of our lives, we need to become a proactive positive author of our choices rather than a spectator.

Think how much of each day we spend in auto-pilot mode. We manage so much in our daily lives out of habit and routine. Let us just look at our last twenty-four hours, reflect on how much of the day has been taken up by routine by things we just do because we do them. We need to break through our boundaries and make time to do all the amazing things of which we have always dreamed.

Complaining is often about not taking responsibility for our lives and not learning from our experiences. When we own our lives and determine the power within us, everything changes. We can reach the point where we wake up in the morning and say, 'I don't want anything more.'

Eckhart Tolle challenges us to look again at both the way we live and the way we are. To be 'present' means to rejoice and delight where you are, being in front of the person here and now. It is the whole of you experiencing the power of life within you as you are in this moment.

Ask yourself:
Who can I forgive?

Can I make my deeds more closely match my values?

How shall I take a little more possession of tomorrow than I had of today?

What small act of kindness can I make tomorrow?

When I speak, what does my body convey? Do I use my hands and my arms?

Some topics for meditation:
The past is no more, the future is not here.
Consider what is now.

I own my present.

Forgiveness

Anger, blame and resentment are heavy burdens.
Let them go, and you become free

To be wronged or hurt is nothing if you don't keep it alive, if you don't feed it energy by remembering it. The only person who suffers when we don't forgive is ourselves, because we carry the anger within us. The best revenge is not to do that. To seek real freedom, let go of the things that chain me. Live forgiveness, be forgiveness and become forgiveness.

Brendan O'Brien is a close friend who worked in Africa for over 40 years. He is a teacher, theologian, expert on African languages and above all a human being who lives his humanity. He has put his life where it matters most and when he left Africa after forty years of giving, he did so as he came, with only the clothes that were on his back. Brendan is loved by everyone and has one of those hearts that embraces you without judgement and without reserve. Brendan shines with gentleness and has a rare sense of fun. I once asked Brendan what he thought was the epicentre of his religion. I asked him what mattered above all else and what was the essence of God. Brendan thought long and hard and looked me gently in the eye. 'Forgiveness...' - he smiled, 'within that there's everything else.' In order to forgive there has to be unrestricted love. Unconditional love is by its nature sacred and through it we find the gateway into true life.

The only person who suffers when we don't forgive is ourselves

Experience often taints and colours our ability to perceive creatively and positively. Stress and tension can slowly build up a web of habits, nothing in particular, but rather the practice of many little things like how we breathe to how we wash our hands. The extent of our experience and our imaginings are the theatre of our lives which often casts shadows on new events, changing them or casting them in a different light.

I was recently talking to a young French journalist about the death toll from malaria that has risen in many parts of Africa. Three Africans die every 60 seconds from malaria and thousands every day become seriously ill. 50,000 per day die from poverty.

Towards the end of the interview Jean noticed my hand as I gestured towards some new possibilities in preventing the spread of new strains of malaria. I was mid-sentence when I noticed that he had started to cry. As he sat helpless, his tears overcame him like a wave. The back of my left hand was badly burnt and the scar became a keloid, it is scarlet and covers the whole hand. As a child, Jean had been looking after his little sister when she fell into a fire and was badly burnt. Her burns left permanent scars - not least on Jean who never forgave himself.

> *Our limited perspective, our hopes and fears become our measure of life, and when circumstances don't fit our ideas, they become our difficulties.*

> Benjamin Franklin

We spend our lives wanting things. True happiness comes not when we get rid of all our problems but when we change our relationship to them.

Most issues can wait their turn to be resolved and what we perceive as stress is merely the result of having been conditioned to accept externally imposed timetables. We are in a culture that has learned to blame and all too often resent. Media creates celebrity only to expose it as human, adulation followed by exploitation, icons of beauty demeaned by the very media that sparked the myth. So too, blame culture seeps into everyday language at school, work and home. Blame is a powerless act. If you see all your decisions as right decisions, it is easier to take responsibility for them. Societies are tribal, dividing us into factions or groups, sub groups and clans, and in these associations we can hide our poor images of ourselves.

There are moments and experiences of ecstasy and wonder, times of wordless wholeness where we feel amazed and fantastic. We can learn to deepen these experiences and fill our lives with delight, joy and pleasure. They are not in things or in drugs or sex, although they can come with tenderness and intimacy. Optimal enjoyment and pleasure is something we can create and learn to experience. These are the moments when we know that this is what life should be about.

This total dynamic involvement makes us get out of bed in the morning and feel so thrilled to be awake, so excited to breathe, and delighted to cele-

True happiness comes not when we get rid of all our problems but when we change our relationship to them.

brate another day. Elated happiness happens when we are in balance with ourselves, and when we see the world through eyes of love.

When you are in love, you are filled by an exhilaration, with a calm, continuous sense of harmony and joy. When this state is how you are all the time, you are in a state of happiness. This is what every human being desires above everything else, to be in a state of joy, dynamic belonging and engagement, a creative energy of goodness and feeling positive about life. It has been called many things: the presence, inner light, enlightenment, flow.

A life full of this continual joy has been touched by love and has become love. It is only in this love that we create from within the power, energy and fire that is happiness. All acts of kindness are inherently wonderful, there is something even more magical about doing something thoughtful and mentioning it to no one, ever.

> *The more genuinely grateful I feel*
> *for the gift of my life, the more*
> *peaceful I feel. Gratitude, then is*
> *worthy of a little practice.*

Richard Carlson

Most of us have to practise.

Ask yourself:
Is there anyone who I have not forgiven?

Is there anyone with whom I am ready to make peace?

Am I holding onto a pain or wound that has

scarred me?

Have I wronged or hurt anyone?

What opportunities do I have to forgive?

Some topics for meditation:
The only people who have hurt me are other suffering people.

Hurt only hurts the one who holds it.

Do I forgive myself?

Becoming through pain and suffering

☾ ☾ ☾ ☾ ☾

Pain comes to us in life, whether we wish it or not. Once we accommodate our own pain, we grow to see others with compassion

We all have times when life hurts. We might be struggling in school, in debt, rejected or bullied. We might feel a little lost or misunderstood, we might be nervous and stressed. Most of the time these things pass. We also can be hurt in other ways, scarred or wounded emotionally, made raw by someone's unkindness or cruelty. There are injuries so profound that they can cripple us, whether in reality or in our imagination. Imaginary damage can be just as real in its physical manifestation. Accident, illness or disability can have a devastating effect on our identity and self-worth

We have a deep longing to be cherished and to belong. Sometimes in life we feel a loss and this loss can become a grief when we feel lonely.

To be lonely is to sense a void within our being, and this can eat away at us until we become crippled and distressed. This alienation sets up a cycle of self-rejection so that we loose contact with the threads of life and nature that can heal us. In this time of darkness it is very hard to see beyond the distress and feelings of emptiness, and towards the light that seems so far away. We all hope that there is someone to hug us, value us and understand us. We all need to be held and appreciated, and if we feel unworthy, or rejected beyond the reach of human love, we become very damaged and isolated.

The gift of life is given to us for a time to convey the energy and power of love, unlocking the vast potential and force within everyone we meet. We were born to be happy and bring joy to those around us in dynamic ways. There are few

We all hope that there is someone to hug us, value us and understand us.

things that we start with so much excitement and desire as being in love, and when it fails we are deeply hurt. The anxieties of these failures can leave us bruised and battered. Life is a succession of crises, when we have to rediscover who we are and what we really want. It is how we engage those challenges that makes the difference. It is how we reach out that creates the change needed, to make the world beautiful. Character cannot be developed in ease and quiet - only through experiencing trial and suffering can the soul be strengthened, ambition inspired, and success achieved.

Negative thought blocks the possibility of growth because it disconnects us from hope. It is only when the forces and powers within awaken that new options and avenues open up within us and real healing can begin deep within the crippled child that is lost in the void. Reclaiming the self takes more than the latest anti-depressant. Recovery requires skilful reconstruction, experienced care and a letting go of the past. Whether in depression, bullying, violence or loss the emotional wasteland is often so blitzed and scarred that healing needs something else, the power of grace and the energy of love. To paraphrase St Francis of Assisi; where there is fear we can bring calm, where there is distress we can bring hope, where there is loneliness we can bring unity and where there is emptiness we can bring wholeness.

Negative thought blocks the possibility of growth because it disconnects us from hope.

Faced with a difficult situation, we may ask ourselves, 'why did this happen to me?', 'what am I going to do?' The negative, disempowering questions produce negative, disempowering answers and feelings of self pity, hopelessness and ultimately even depression. When we ask positive, empowering questions like 'what can I learn from this?' or, 'How can I let go of this?' we open ourselves to a different set of emotions. Most of us experience fear and stress. We have times of anxiety and loneliness. We do not know the wounds that have scarred other people's hearts.

One of my friends is successful and popular, and a very gifted artist. Peter is handsome, educated, funny and is wonderful company. He said, 'I was first diagnosed with depression when I was in my 2nd year at school, and started taking pills at the end of it, that's when I became anorexic as well. It was absolutely horrible; I always thought I was fat, I remember I went into a shop and nothing fitted me, they had to give me women's trousers I had a 27 inch waist back then I think. It lasted for ages. I wouldn't eat and when I did it was only like a couple of bites. I remember I was at my cousin's house for her birthday and the food looked amazing and all I wanted to do was eat and eat but I wouldn't let myself. What stopped me was when one morning my mum cooked me breakfast but I wouldn't eat and left the room, she ran into the back garden and had a semi break down so I gave myself a slap across the face and saw what it was doing to my mum and my family.

'I thought then that I would eat but work out after every time I ate, so I would not gain anything. That was a bad idea too, because now nearly nine or ten years later I am still addicted to working out. Most anorexics and people who think they are fat or with low self-esteem do. You wouldn't have recognised me then, I was a totally different person.

'I love going away on my own, I inevitably end up having war with myself when I do, and I always discover some part of me that I didn't know was there. I went down to Kerry on a two week art residency. It was the most remote place I had ever been, ten miles from the nearest village. It was on a cliff on the Atlantic, next stop New York. A thousand foot mountain chain was my back drop. To stop the voices in my head I would go running. The first three days were hell, you couldn't see beyond your finger, literally, because of the mist. My parents were staying in Killarney for a few nights, they said that they would call in to me on their way home. I remember though, when I saw them, it felt like they were coming to see me in a mental hospital or a prison.

We can become prisoners of our own misery, of our own illusions.

'They saw me for an hour, took me out to see the outside world, and dropped me back to the four walls. It comforted me that they were slowly becoming my friends. I was going to name them, I would talk to them. But then suddenly when I went for my run up the mountain, the mist lifted and I didn't even realise I was so gone. I had dived so far into my own head, I forgot that the world still turned. I remember being absolutely blown away by it, my surroundings were out of this world, the sunset, the colours the little village that I lived in with the six strangers doing their own arty thing, were there. I knew then that I had to do this; I couldn't let myself struggle with myself anymore. I had to paint. I went manic in a good way. My paintings were whacky and I loved them, they all sold. The joy that I felt there I can't express as I cry every time. The two best weeks of my life – I cried, feared, laughed, I felt wanted.'

For several years I have corresponded with two people in very different circumstances. One, let's call him Jay, is a 35 year old man who lost a leg in a car accident while in high school. The other is a 23 year old girl who had both legs blown of by a land mine at her school when she was 15; let's call her Sue. Every communication with Jay has always been in relation to his disability. He remains trapped in regret and anger, his accident has been the cause of all his problems and arguments, people fail to understand him, he had his life ruined and he has difficulty seeing himself as whole without his limb. His grief continues to block other opportunities and each refusal to challenge himself is rationalised by the tragedy that befell him. Sue is now a teacher, she walks from her home to the village school on prosthetic legs and has in every way a full and complete life; she has a young daughter and a husband. She has never defined herself by her disability or as a victim, but rather as a person with the freedom of choice. We can become trapped in the way we recall experience.

We can become prisoners of our own misery, of our own illusions.

When reflecting on personal pain, we all have memories, moments, experiences to draw on. It is healthy to identify where our wounds came from, and to learn from how we have managed them. We can learn to think about pain differently, in a way that frees us from being hurt even more.

EPIC PAIN

Epic pain is tragedy on an immense scale; the recent genocides of Sudan and Rwanda, earthquakes across Asia, the Tsunami in December 2004, hurricane Katrina in New Orleans. Epidemics and floods, droughts and mindless cruelty; sadly there are too many examples of brutality, natural and man made.

I have worked in disaster areas and times of human anguish, when it is easy to lose one's way and easy to forget that there is goodness in this world. We humans have shown endless invention in finding new ways to destroy each other and ourselves. We see only clearly when we can see beyond cruelty and injustice. There will always be greed and apathy, the powerful will crush the weak, and there will be injustice to confound all reason. We can cry and be broken by the absurdities, or do everything we can to create new opportunities. Unless we pour love into times of hate, there will only be more hate.

When terrible things happen we can despair, or respond to needs and heal wounds. Pain has many masks. It is anything that destroys, violates, murders peace in a single life or in many lives; it is all that is dreadful, horrific, cruel, tragic and unkind in creation.

Loving and caring is beautiful but life is more than beautiful thoughts and compassion. When I wrote *All Will be Well*, a number of people said that life definitely was not OK, that the world was torn apart and that there is cruelty and evil in the world. This, of course, is true. The world is a battlefield, polarised and fragmented. The poor become poorer and the rich grow more cynical. There is darkness in the world and cruelty on a scale that defies understanding. In *All Will be Well*, many stories illustrating the evil side of humanity were edited out, considered too dark for a general audience. As we go through life, our experience of pain and suffering separate into two kinds, the things that happen to us as individuals and the things that happen to others.

Unless we pour love into times of hate, there will only be more hate.

Understanding the power we can have over life's disasters and cruelty frees us from some of the prisons that pain can create. This realisation is the beginning of the journey of the Tao and the secret of becoming.

Death is our becoming and our fullness, the drawing together of all we truly are, the love that we have given. It is when we become light. It is the power within us, united and transformed into conscious energy. It is our last selves and our first selves united into a greater light.

> *Death is no more than passing from*
> *one room into another. But there's a*
> *difference for me, you know.*
> *Because in that other room I shall*
> *be able to see.*

Helen Keller

One of the keys to surviving fear and sorrow is the same as the key to being fully alive. It is knowing that, 'this too shall pass.' In our deepest despair and greatest loneliness, we can loose sight of everything, consumed by our anguish and emptiness. Whether we have been rejected or lost a loved one, been betrayed or deeply hurt, it can be hard to see any goodness in ourselves or see any redemption. There is a common thread between people who have been deeply injured. Whether tortured or falsely accused, watching their children die or being utterly alone, we are in our darkness, blind to reason, unable to think, raw, and void of the most basic sense. The only notion with any shred of meaning in the face of cruelty and meaningless suffering is compassion. It is best without words of advice, it is simply silent presence. After 9/11 and the aftermath, there was a flurry of speeches, rage promises of revenge and anger. When Bill Clinton visited the families, the only thing he did was to embrace them, no words, no assurances, no advice, just embrace. In the face of great suffering, the greatest eloquence is in simply holding someone's hand in their dying, being with them through the night, being simply human. We do not have explanations or reasons, there is often no logic or purpose to what happens to us, but in the face of overwhelming grief, we can simply be there.

In my work the most important thing is often to be silent and simply be human, sharing the journey of another. In grief all we have is our shared humanity. While I can do everything practically possible to ease the death of a mother, secure a future for her children, protect their future, there is so often little I can do for her fears and anxieties, the torment of leaving her hungry children behind in a dangerous world. It is only grace and the presence of love that can calm such fears, forces greater than ourselves that can ease such darkness.

Death is our becoming and our fullness, the drawing together of all we truly are, the love that we have given.

I have seen many children die in famines and droughts, epidemics and conflict. Most have died with a calmness, it is adults who have often died torn and divided, afraid to leave the world that has not treated them as well as they deserve. One woman recently was dying, having buried her three children in the midst of, yes, another famine. All of them died from dehydration. She told me that she was happy to be going to be with her children where the angels would not let them starve and she spat on the ground and said that in this world with so much of everything, the humans in it could not find enough to let her children eat so why stay here. I have no answer to the injustice

It is obvious that we should make our planet a better place to live.

and perversions of a world so wrong. The greed of the few will perhaps be looked on in history as the worst of genocides with fifty thousand dying each day. I have no answer, yet the way to change the poverty around us is easy; those who have the wealth must share it, not waste it making wars. The pet food expenditure of the United Kingdom could provide enough food to prevent the famine in East Africa and the cosmetic expenditure of the USA could provide all the funding it would take to eradicate poverty.

I do not have answers to the injustices or the dramas we face, other than with every breath in my body to try and change the evil of the present. Providing basic Human Rights is not an act of charity, it is simply being human.

Until we change from looking at the poor as another or a sub-species, and embrace them as part of our own family, our response will continue to fail. Until we rethink the misery industry, until we all intervene directly against the suffering of the poor, wealthy charities and the lords of poverty will carry on flying first class over the deserts of the starving.

It is a sad comment on our mass of celebrities, that the ones who really use their influence to challenge what is wrong are the few, not the many. It is a sadder comment on media, politicians and the electorate, that the greatest atrocities and genocides are relegated behind local and parochial issues. Until we see ourselves as world citizens, we will be limiting our concerns to our neighbourhood.

Changing the world is an issue, it is something that should not be a cause or philanthropy, it has nothing to do with charity or being nice. It is simply the nature of being human! It is obvious that we should make our planet a better place to live, obvious that we should clothe the naked and protect the vulnerable. It is primary to care for the sick, and how we treat the mentally ill defines our society. So too, our humaneness is defined in how we care for those who are not surviving in our world. A teenage footballer in Dublin and a Banker in Canary Wharf share the same responsibility as the boy carrying his starved sister into a clinic in the northern deserts of Africa. I am not my brother's keeper, but I definitely am my brother's brother.

Whether our biggest worry tonight is our mortgage repayments, our angry boss or our broken iPod, we have no less an obligation to humanity than the woman carrying water on her back to her sick neighbour in the slums of Sào Paolo. Tonight there are over ninety million people who will sleep without food, in a world of food mountains. Surely, we cannot allow this to continue. There are a thousand reasons why we do not do enough, why we do nothing and how we reason our indifference. In the

I am not my brother's keeper, but I definitely am my brother's brother.

end we make a choice; we can close the book, switch the channel on the television... or we can decide to make a difference. No matter who you are, you can change the world.

I met a journalist in Ireland, Joe Humphries of the Irish Times. We sat outside a closed pub and we shared a couple of hours before I caught a flight to India. Joe wrote an article about the work ICROSS is doing in Africa. That article started waves of responses that allowed us to reach thousands more AIDS orphans and many thousands of vulnerable children in need of health care. That one single article created many opportunities that touched the lives of people in dozens of communities across Africa.

Months later we were contacted by RTE, the main Irish TV station. The award winning broadcaster Jim Fahy had read Joe Humphries' article and wanted to come with a film crew to see for himself the realities

Joe had written about. For weeks the film crew filmed in the desert and the remote villages of East Africa in what became a labour of love. Joe had started a chain reaction and Jim created a documentary which in turn touched many people and shared the courage and struggle of many African mothers and children, crippled by extremes of poverty. The film changed the realities of thousands of African victims of AIDS and allowed many people to touch the lives of others, helping to lift them out of poverty, towards a better day.

Ask yourself:
Has anger been in my way?

Do I acknowledge what frightens or hurts me?

How can I begin to accept the pain I encounter?

If I encounter suffering, what shall I do about it?

A topic for meditation:
What can pain teach?

Inspiration

Inspiration transforms wishes into action

Faced with the inevitable pressures and suffering that life throws into our path, it is easy to become hurt or overwhelmed. As we go through life, however, we are often guided along the way, we are moved sometimes by the majesty of creation, at other times by amazing music. Above all, I think we are most enriched by other people who inspire us. Reflecting on this, I asked a few friends a simple question. I chose people I knew across the globe, and over a wide age group, from monks to sex workers, from teenagers to some in their later years. Read their answers and think of your own gut response. The answers are important and form the basis of my next reflection. I asked my friends, '*what inspired, touched and lifted you?*'

Dr Don Kilby is famous in Canada for his work in AIDS. He wrote about inspiration, 'Nothing inspires me more than children. No matter where you are in the world, children have a yet unspoiled innocence that reminds us of where we have all come from. We were all once totally innocent, open to others, unaware of what separates us. Children are unspoiled by the prejudice, hatred and misconceptions that will eventually define their world. If a child who I hold in my arms can accept me, even love me without question, without knowing who I am or where I am from, then I, who am less vulnerable, can also exchange love and trust with strangers and acquaintances. Bring on the children, let them teach us how to see the world as it is and as it can be, to love as only a child can love and explore the wonders that surround us all.'

Ron Nelson in Washington said, 'In my adventures, travels, education, readings, and listening to others, I have come to find wonder and awe in the simplest of things. I cringe at harm done to people and animals. I cringe at wonton destruction of nature and marvel at the structure of a flower petal and the beat of the hummingbird's wings at my feeder at the window. I find joy at the surf, the rays of sunrise and the glory of sunset. I am amazed at the complexity of my body parts, their functions and how it keeps me breathing and walking, and at the same time I wonder how an ant can lift so much weight. I cannot understand killing another human, but know war on a personal level. I see God in every religion and no religion. I am idealistic to my own detriment most times. Why? I detest doing wrong to

What inspires, touches and lifts you?

others. Doing the right thing has always been the clear path. How do I come by this? I am a romantic. I am stubborn. I hate how self-righteous I can be....because I know I am not. I appreciate the beauty in all things. I hope this makes some sense to you.'

Another friend said, 'Seeing a little child smile at me is uplifting. People who are passionate about something, and who follow their dreams, touch me deeply. Certain music is like honey for my soul; it must come from God. A friend from years ago helped change things for me. U2 music is like a drug for me. Being raised poor has helped me see things differently. My Mom's death from cancer has affected me. Looking into my wife's eyes when we are intimate is amazing. Why? Why does thinking of my daughter, when she was three, smiling up at me, freeze me? Why does music uplift and sometimes motivate? Why does a person hurting another person make me cry or want to seek revenge? Why am I so afraid to follow my passions? Answer these, and you will be nothing short of amazing.'

Lisa is a girl who came to work in one of our AIDS programmes in Africa; she said, 'God, honesty, love, serenity, childbirth, giving birth, a baby, my children, family, friends, sunsets, stars, ocean air, sun shining through snow or ice covered trees, nature, the unknown, spirituality, the warmth of the sun, flowers, a beautiful song, voice & music, both of my daughters' singing, stories of angels, nice memories, a fire's flame, reading a book that touches my soul, people who make this earth a kinder place, people who work together, the innocence of children, intelligent people, devotedness, compassion, weakness, older kind and loving couples, people with disabilities, new discoveries, progress, laughter, family, writing poetry, witnessing acts of kindness, reaching a deeper connection with someone, sharing emotions with

"People who are passionate about something, and who follow their dreams, touch me deeply."

another, making a new friend, technology - exchanging e-mails with people in other countries that otherwise you would never speak to, meet or converse with, spending time with an elderly person you love, moments of emotion and raw truth in life, helping people, learning new things, finding places of peace, finding peace within yourself, finding wisdom...that lifts me.'

Jamie, a very successful business man, said, 'What inspires me? I am quite a selfish person so probably all my answers would be rather bland and superficial, I regret. I often think about doing more and Africa really inspires me, I love being there and although I normally go there for work reasons (business/money) I love the people, rawness of stepping off that plane and being on my own, travelling around. I have now visited most of Africa many times and I love going back. Africa has a distinct smell that

I can't describe; either you've tasted it or you will never know. Is it the heat, humidity, dirt...?'

The author Tessa McWatt wrote, 'Many things inspire me, touch me and lift me, but if I had to distil the essence of those many things, it would come down to a sense of "magic," of creative forces behind things like art. My eyes were opened up by my deep partnership with an artist. He didn't have words, the way I have, he had a whole other dimension of the universe, and I tapped into it through him. Art seems like magic when it works, because it is about the unsayable, the unspeakable. It's about layering the stories of human experience and in the layering, there is some kind of truth. It's magic because it imbues objects – paint, plaster, metal, books, celluloid, cellos, CDs – with spirit. And when it can do that, it's always a surprise, which touches the same place and creates the same joy. I have learned that every single act, every word, every thing we do, every thing we eat, has an aesthetic value and is imbued with a sense of magic if we are conscious of it. Aesthetics are magic because they transcend the things in which they are embedded. Children are the same – magic. Nature is the same – magic. Love is the same – magic. So, on a technical level: Love, Art, Nature – that "holy" trinity for me – all of them

I am inspired by the overwhelming grace that shines within people and the countless miracles every day.

showing that the whole is much greater than the sum of the parts. That's when I smile.'

Pizir is a crippled child who lives beside a railway track in Mumbai. He said, 'I'm inspired by people who are kind and if they are nice to me and do not hurt me. I am touched if people smile at me because they see me as worth smiling at.'

Christina is a single mother in Swansea. 'I am inspired by music and by my children, seeing how they can be excited by little things. How content they are with each other and when they look at me, and I am there for them, the most important thing in their world as they are everything in mine.'

A pattern seems to form in what moves us. In answering this question myself, I find inspiration flooding into my life from two directions, like two great waterfalls drowning every pain and fear in the power of their flow. Firstly, I am inspired by the overwhelming grace that shines within people and the countless miracles every day. I am constantly thrilled and amazed by the extraordinary goodness within people and the awakening of hope within them.

Children, and the magical bond they have with delight, inspire me, gentleness and compassion which is everywhere excites me and the perennial capacity to love and to give, touches my heart and encourages me. Every tiny act of kindness and love is a lasting inspiration. The many people I have mentioned in these pages inspire me, the Sharons, Elles, Tom Hogans, Joe Barnes', Ronán Conroys continue to fill my life with raw joy. They each bring pleasure, laughter and light every day.

The second stream of power that overwhelms everything for me is in the very fabric of each breath. It is the primordial fire that binds us to each other and to eternity. It is the constant presence of grace, energy flowing through us despite our frailty, power surging through us with such clarity. It is the silent presence of the abyss, the heaving of the universe, the

Children, and the magical bond they have with delight, inspire me.

real and total presence of the hidden. In silence we give space for ourselves to be conscious of this still fire, but it is this presence that is the origin of all else, it is this one single force that unites everything into completeness and harmony. The most profound inspiration is the state of being aware of this light within us. Reflecting its perfection is all that has been created from the heaving of the cosmos and the hum of the universe. It is the realisation that in everything there is a drawing together and a chaos transformed into stillness. There is in all of the visible absurdity around us, a single unity that is not always obvious. This inspiration is simply the presence of the origin of joy, the purest centre and most dynamic becoming. It is the presence of love in our lives. Its voice is compassion, its words are stillness, its heart beat is mystery and we have tried to name it from the dawn of time. By whatever name, it is pure love.

Ask yourself:
What stimulates me?

What inspired me this month?

Who encourages me?

Where can these inspirations lead me?

A topic for meditation:
What are my goals?

CHANGE

See past the darkness that is, to the light that can be, and change becomes possible

It is fantastic to be inspired, but does inspiration help us to become? Are there lessons that can enrich us as well as touch us? Experiences such as music, art, books and our culture, shape how we behave. The drama of life runs around us with surprises, new tastes, twists and uncertainties. And sometimes we are uplifted, touched and moved by those around us. I asked some friends about the inspirations that have changed them.

The things that lift and inspire us do so by enriching the way we see life itself. Children, music, art, creation, renewal, heroism, grace, these are energies greater than ourselves, calling us further, awakening something in us. When we are inspired there is wonder, we see hope and new life. Being inspired changes what we are because it teaches us something about ourselves in a very real way.

It is that 'something' that is the seed of delight and purpose, the more we learn to use this energy the more it can permeate our lives, the more we learn to become inspired.

Don Kilby said, 'My father was a simple self-taught man who worked hard, had a difficult childhood and who believed that it is only in loving and caring for others that we can grow. We were taught to do something good for someone else everyday; never to speak of the good we did for others and to perform our deeds, when possible, so that not even the benefactor would know it had been done by us. Never have I experienced so much love and compassion

When we are inspired there is wonder, we see hope and new life.

as I experienced with him. Though he grew to be successful, he only did so because he believed that if a job was worth doing, it was worth doing right. And he so loved children, and they so loved him, like the children of Hamelin following the Pied Piper, they flocked to him. Of probably equal inspiration was my grandmother (not my father's as she died when my father was 14). This mother of 10 lived to be 99 years old. She was a strong matriarch, not so much as how she ruled over her family as how she shouldered the burdens of her children, grandchildren and great-grandchildren. She gave unconditional love and encouragement. There was no such thing for her as a bad child, and we remained her children well into our adult lives. She saw the good in everyone, even the 'fallen' and all felt her welcome. We felt her sincerity as she focused on our qualities and strengths and ignored our weaknesses. I have been blessed many times over. I was born to wonderful parents, into a great family of uncles and aunts and cousins. I remained healthy all my life, I chose the best possible career for myself, and I was born in a country where anyone can achieve their hopes. Most of all I am blessed that I have retained my capacity for love.'

The drama of life runs around us with surprises, new tastes, twists and uncertainties.

Another friend said, 'In growing up, my ideals came from observing my parents and their interactions with each other, friends, relatives, my brother and myself. My mother taught me respect for other people, and never, never speak badly of people, or badly to them. I observed a lot of inner strength in her and learned a type of reasoning from how she reasoned, how to see people or situations created by people, and depend on my gut instincts about them. Kindnesses I have received from others have forever stayed with me.'

Another answer was, 'Who has changed me? Surprisingly both good and not so good people come to mind, i.e. the terrible devastation on September 11th brought a strong desire to people, myself included, to do more good, to be kinder, in a way somehow to bring more light to erase the darkness of that day. Reading or hearing about terrible things that happen to people has made me much more compassionate in life towards other people. Moments of personal devastation have caused the most change in my life, but has also brought me the most growth and has led me to a truer reality outside of what society teaches, and to know my true strengths and desires i.e. a failed marriage. Immigrants at my work have touched me. I am amazed at their bravery to leave their home to come to a strange country and in some cases not know the language or know anyone.

'This inspired me to volunteer with an organization in which I sponsored an immigrant with friendship, and this experience opened my eyes to a new culture. My children have affected my life immensely and bring me continued amazement. I am blessed to have three great children. It is an experience to raise three children from birth. They have affected the way I see things and life, they made me experience things in life all over again, made me see things truthfully, innocently and taught me many things about myself.

My sister, who was once extremely ill and recovered, and my father, who had a two-year illness before his death, made me see life as something much more precious and helped me find a deeper appreciation of my health and the health of my children. He was a kind and loving man, and a great father. Another inspiration that changed me is a mother's love; my mother, who leaves me almost without words to describe the impact and importance of her undying love, kindness and strength in my life. To know this in life is a true blessing and I could not bear to think what my life would have been like without her.

'I think everyone we meet in life touches us in some way, some at deeper levels than others, some good and bad, all teaching us new things. I have met a tremendous number of people in my life through work and through friends, and have learned just as much about myself as I have of them. I enjoy people but enjoy times of solitude immensely.'

Lisa replied, 'When I think of an AIDS worker I know in Kenya, Francis Mwangi in Nakuru, and how he has taken in 7 young orphan boys and made them his family, that inspires me and reassures me. When I think of my boyfriend, and how he continues to love me and be gentle to me no matter how much I might try to fight it, that touches me. When I think of my friends in Ngong - and how we felt as comfortable together as my I do with my friends in Toronto, that touches me. Really special, once you see for yourself how people around the world are the same. When I see pure good in people, that lifts me. When I see my aunts and uncles try to break old layers that they've built that actually stifle them, that inspires me. When I think of what I learned from reading Nelson Mandela's autobiography, I am inspired and in awe.'

Stefan is a rent boy from Warsaw working in London who was recently badly beaten up, 'I am inspired by the last Pope. He was shot, broken, hurt, he saw Poland crushed and showed us what it means to have no fear. He would go at night to take young men out of the police station as bishop in Krakow, and never left without them because he knew they would be tortured. When his body fell apart and he could not speak properly he still loved us and spoke to us, and from his soul he told us to be strong. Then when he could not raise his hands to wave he had someone raise him up and hold his hand to bless us, in the end only his eyes showed who he was. His presence, even in a ruined body, was enough. Is this what you mean when you say inspired?'

'I think everyone we meet in life touches us in some way.'

Francesca is an 82 year old Italian nurse who has spent over fifty years in Africa, 'Near where I grew up there was a girl, she was born blind, she was a dwarf and very crippled. She was an outcast and rejected by her family. Margherita Benedetta del Castello was a beggar. She is the patron of the rejected and the outcast, the unwanted and the hated. As a child she was my heroine, I can't imagine a human being more inspiring, she cared for the lost and the unwanted.'

Morten Skovdal is a young Danish health professional who works with me in Africa. Everyone he meets is warmed by his gentleness, his burning passion to care, and they are inspired by his quiet determination to make a difference in this hurting world. He does it with an unspoken clarity and tenderness.

My guardian angel is a woman called Sharon who I have known since I was young. Sharon always responded to a crisis by starting with the solution while other friends would panic at the fallout or what else might go wrong. While some dramatised emergencies, Sharon had charted the way forward. Sharon is a party girl, everything is a celebration, and she is usually laden down wherever she travels, mostly with gifts, surprises and special things for special people. To Sharon, everyone is a miracle, even the time wasters, they all have something wonderful.

Kimotho Gathoni was a young African who loved life. He was a close friend, and we were inseparable. His children played while he worked and he had many children. He lived with a voracious appetite for everything and he was an infusion of bliss, elation, ecstasy and delight. Kimotho had a sparkle in his eye and in a decade I had never seen him without a smile. We worked with children who were often lost and alone, hurt and vulnerable. Kimotho lit up every child and worked magic with them. He would love the most broken child and somehow from somewhere within him came something that cast away their fears and terrors. He possessed the rarest power with them simply because he was as one of them. Kimotho never believed in rules and lived on the edge. Kimotho died suddenly in a swimming pool accident, and I was unprepared for the darkness that followed. The loss of so a great a spirit left me shattered and dazed, and it was Sharon and David Wilkinson who held me through the void. I do not believe that we should ever get used to suffering or that we should harden to it. I hope I never harden or fail to cry when faced with things we should cry about. Some people enrich and bless us. The Elles of this world generate limitless happiness, abundant joy. They are delight, possessed with what matters, incarnations of the force from which we flow.

Changing everything begins with the little choices in the only moment we can control; the 'now'.

There have been moments in my life when I was crushed, times when I have been utterly bereft and clouded with sorrow, Sharon was there. When I felt alone and tired, Sharon was there and when I was drained she would come to me. She held my hand when I was about to have an operation and accepts my many vanities. She has seen my frailty, and cherished it when I condemned it.

We are in constant evolution which is the synergy of experiences. We have spoken of selfhood, the path to self-celebration. It is simply a way of life that embraces gentleness and chooses to cope with life by creating opportunities and new ways of seeing problems.

We spoke of the way others can influence us and the power of wonder which creates in us renewal and healing. We reflected on how this becoming can happen now, not in some future enlightenment. Changing everything begins with the little choices in the only moment we can control, the 'now.'

We have spoken of forgiveness and the need to rethink our perception of pain and suffering, channelling our energies through inspiration and creative loving.

We always strive towards wholeness, to be complete, to be at one with our innermost being. At the core of our being is our individual spiritual essence. This essence is pure love and it is protected and guarded so as not to come to harm. The secret is to have confidence enough to release this inner core and let it permeate through our whole being: the calmness, silence, listening and compassion.

Ask yourself:
What makes me happy?

Who has touched my heart?

Some topics for meditation:
A better day.

I am the author of my life.

What can I change, here and now?

Calm

*In calmness, and only in calmness, we connect
with our true self*

All of us know people in our lives who radiate calmness. We have seen people who by their nature instil peace around them. Simply by being there, they can transform the energy of a room. As we live, we absorb and give off energy. Some people fill a room with their joy, others with their stress; we spread the energy that we create. So too, this tranquillity and calm changes those around us and generates more calm.

Willie Nyambati is a friend and we work together in Africa. I have seen him in many situations dealing with conflicts, crises, emergencies and ordinary every-day problems. While those around him often panic in the face of emergencies, Willie invariably responds deliberately. His presence slows people in their rush and his voice slows their agitation. He is by nature in such possession of his own energy that he is untroubled by the distress around him. He brings calm and peace to difficult situations, which enables people to listen to each other and find solutions. Through the respect he has for his own being, he is able to share the energy of that balance with those who have no calm of their own. Calmness is not a state that exists only in solitude and monastic retreat, it should thrive in the midst of life with all its surprises and profusion, all its contradiction and drama.

My close friend Father Albert, a Cistercian Trappist, once said, 'Never let anything reduce your inner calm, we cannot edit the sacred or reduce our inner silence for anything. Never let anyone close to you who could in any way reduce this, because this is where you meet the presence of God, and nothing should invade your inner life, if it does, separate yourself from it.' I have tried to live by this wisdom and have always sensed overwhelming freedom because of this insight.

Sorrow is part of life. We will always come across bullies and tyrants, demanding people and those who hate our guts. That may never change.

Inner calm is found in reflection and contemplation.

Yet we will also meet others who heal us,

raise us up. People who know how to transform stress into enjoyable challenges, those who spend little time thinking about themselves. Inner calm is found in reflection and contemplation. You don't need to study the Cistercian Trappists or Tibetan monks to understand this path, it is inborn in us. My own background introduced me early in life to the Spanish mystic Teresa of Avila, and to the writings of the mystics and contemplatives. Others might be more familiar with the rich and ancient traditions of Vedic knowledge or Buddhist and Taoist schools. The more we study, the more we see that the internal power of these wisdoms is the same. The language differs; the parables and cryptic semiotics vary as do the cosmology and model, but the centre is the same.

No matter how fantastic life is, we need down time.

If we want to find balance within ourselves, we need time for detachment, time and space where we disconnect from the race and drama of life. No matter how fantastic life is, we need down time. We need regular spiritual and emotional maintenance, deleting the unnecessary from our minds, clearing out the trash that slows us down

Our thoughts should lead to the things that bring us wonder, hope, delight, joy, love. They should channel energy towards grace, turn our minds from worry, fear, sadness and depression. The more we practise, the easier it gets. Teresa of Avila said, 'Let nothing disturb you, let nothing frighten you, all things are passing, love alone is changeless, patience gains all things, who has love wants for nothing, love alone is changeless.'

Calmness allows you to connect with power that you never knew you had. When others expect you to be as frustrated as they are, be calm. A colleague talked about a perceived difficulty, and she grew clearly upset and annoyed when I rejected her anxiety. When we are annoyed or frustrated we get angry and confrontational, but conflict cannot occur unless we choose to engage it. Just as I cannot be insulted unless I bend down to pick up the insult, I cannot be drawn into a row unless I decide to cease being calm. Buddhism teaches to part from people who approach life as a series of conflicts.

We do not need agitated energies around us, and should avoid them. It is possible to live without the head butt approach and be successful. There is nothing effective, decent or helpful in the philosophies that masquerade as direct, honest business techniques. Many of the accepted behaviours in modern business are neither honourable nor compassionate, and only serve to damage the grace of love in the world. We must not sacrifice our spirit on the altar of expediency, or sell out our way of life for cash. A good acid test is to ask ourselves, 'Will this path be within my inner grace? Does it accord with my values? Is it within my spirit?'

I once asked Lemoite, one of my adopted Samburu sons, why he was always so peaceful. He did not understand the question and after I explained it carefully he looked at me with his magical smile and thought for a long time. After a few hours walking with the camels we breed, he offered a thought, and here is a direct translation; 'If you belong here and know you're here then you're here but maybe if you think you should be somewhere else, you won't be here then you'll be in two places. Here where you don't want to be, and there where you'll never be.' He went on, 'People think too much and their brains get too full, and there's not enough space left to stop thinking and be what you're meant to be. You should think only about little things, and the big things you do with your heart.' Then he was silent again for a long time, totally at peace with the Samburu great Rift, the camels and the sunset.

It took the vastness of the African sky and the scale of the firmament to stage the kaleidoscope of colours that appeared, the rays of light exploded in a symphony of reds and oranges each shining in a million bolts across the primeval landscape. I looked for my camera; Lemoite was still and raised his head to the setting sun.

Ask yourself:
Might I be less clumsy, or perhaps more effective, if I slowed down a little?

In social situations, do I take a dominant or a passive role? How would it be if I took a different position?

Is my voice peaceful?

How much space have I made for myself this week, to be peaceful, alone with myself?

What area of my life can I make calmer?

A topic for meditation:
The Breathing meditation (see page 38).

Silence

*Silence is the space where we can receive
our true self*

One thing that will free us from the frenetic anxieties of modern life is finding stillness to restore us. Changing ourselves and those around us requires space and time for calmness, silence and stillness. Each day some, however little, each day a little more. As this practice grows, so we too will grow.

We have spent our lives reinforcing habits. We automatically become unhappy, angry, hurt and frustrated, because we learned to, long ago. We may have accepted that behaviour and never challenged it, but we can learn not to be unhappy, angry, or frustrated just as we learned to be all those self-defeating things. This is what we can learn within our stillness, in the midst of our lives. Practising inner stillness does not take a long time, it is something we reconnect with, it is already within us.

Silence is one of the most important things in my life. It is my time for restoration, where the fires are lit and rekindled, and energies are drawn together. It is more of a way of life than a practice; it is a habit that becomes so a part of me, it is like my breathing. More intimate than sexual union, more powerful than creeds, more healing than medicines, the power of inner stillness is essential to self-discovery. The ways of the early mystics and the sacred arts of ancient rites are steeped in it. It is the language of the old monastic Orders and Lamas, it is the very gate to the ways of Oneness. Silence is not about the mind but a state of inner awareness of what is; silence is the reality of the nature of who we are and what we are. For millennia, the wise have written about the paths of silence and inner stillness, and the saints have lost themselves in its embrace. Those who changed us spoke its language and everyone from the Buddha and Sun Tzu

It is love alone that will complete and heal us.

to Mandela and Ghandi drew wisdom from its well. It has many names in many scriptures, dreamed of and longed for. It is the fire of Zen and the breath of the Tao. It is the path of silence, of inner stillness. 'The more a man is united within himself and interiorly simple, the more and higher things doth he understand without labour; because he receiveth the light of understanding from above.' Thomas à Kempis

For me what works is an hour of Hatha Yoga at midnight, then a couple of hours of stillness, usually in darkness or with a single candle. Sometimes when travelling this might be difficult which is why I choose the middle of the night or early morning since these are times without interruption. When small children are around, the only time to be silent is when they are asleep. Sleeping habits improve when we calm ourselves, breathe slowly and calmly, let go of distractions and fears, cast out imaginings and listen to the breath of our bodies.

> *Only when one is connected to one's*
> *inner core, is one connected to*
> *others... And, for me, the core, the*
> *inner spring, can best be re-found*
> *through solitude.*

Anne Morrow Lindbergh

There is something rejuvenating and peaceful about being alone and getting time to reflect, work or simply enjoy the quiet, because the greatest revelation is stillness. Stillness is only transforming if it lives rooted in daily reality; it is self-deception if it is not woven into our day. Unless our spirituality is part of each minute of action, it is illusion. Stillness within silence is not enough. Only when there is stillness in movement can the spiritual rhythm appear which permeates the whole of our lives. Everything will pass away, every building, car and road will eventually finish, all we see will pass except stillness.

We can commune with the essential; because we are part of the light. It is love alone that will complete and

Sleeping habits improve when we calm ourselves.

heal us. Restored in our deeper being we sense a whole that is greater than ourselves, a belonging that has no words or reason. This is where we leave intellect and leap into the brightness of the cloud of unknowing, the cloud of forgetting. This state of stillness holds an energy that has been written about for centuries in every culture. It is the place where we meet the invisible. In inner unity everything finds a harmony no matter how torn the world might be around us.

Here we can unite in the height, depth, length and breadth of creation without words, only the voice of our hearts. This type of inner stillness is not technique, it is grace. When we empty our mind of distraction and constant activity we gain a sense of emptiness, an awareness at a profound level of nothingness. It is here in this presence that we experience a union with all creation. We realise that our junk, our egos and the things that busy us, are not so important.

This awareness is felt, not reasoned. This inner discovery is one of the most powerful forces within us.
Our lives are wonderfully changed when we connect
to this spiritual experience. Discovering this energy
inside us changes the way we see ourselves and everything around us; it is a transforming life changing
process, it's not about a faith, but about awakening
to the power of life within you and the grace of love
that delights in us. It is, above all, the frightening
realisation that despite ourselves, we are loved from
before the dawn of time. We are known, we are celebrated, we are miracles. To me it is overwhelming,
exciting and awesome, that here in an inner silence,
and that the heaving of the universe and the hymn of
creation is enfolded within us. For this there are
many names. People like to name things but as the
fox said in Antoine de Saint-Exupéry's *The Little
Prince*, 'It is only with the heart that one sees rightly,
what is essential is invisible to the eye.'

We can all carve out some tiny space each day for
ourselves. This is one of the most important and
transforming gifts we can give ourselves. It is a
luxury that enriches us the more we do it. We often
deceive ourselves into thinking that we do not have
enough time to be silent or to let go. It is when we
are most pressured and busy that we have the greatest need for this silence. One of the benefits of living
among nomads is that they are very comfortable with
quietness; they are very content around silence and
peaceful in the midst of total stillness.

Ask yourself:
*What could I do to be more comfortable
with myself?*

A topic for meditation:
Energy in stillness.

Listening

*Being listened to and heard is one
of the greatest desires of the human
heart.*

Richard Carlson

My closest friends are all women, all those I confide in are women and all who know me in my whole humanity and still accept me are women. I think women are often better listeners. It is like Sharon, an act of utter surrender, willingly cherishing another's world and embracing the whole consciousness of the other. But when Sharon does so, it is never with feigned excitement, never with fake interest, it is with her total pleasure filled being.

I have seen Sharon with irritating bureaucrats, her wonderful sons and their girlfriends, I have seen her with her Mum and sisters and with her wonderful husband. I am always in awe of her gift to listen, listen within, listen inside the words, beyond the meaning, into the heart. When I listen I sometimes think too much and feel too little.

Many people are never by themselves. As one young man said to me through hot tears of frustration and anger, 'it's just I really can't bear being alone, by myself, I just really hate my life. I hate me.' His problem was not actually that he hated himself, but he was frustrated with the emptiness and bore-dom that seemed to flood in along with the pressures and demands placed on him. Like many young people, he felt constantly told what he was doing wrong, always controlled, hassled, forced to perform and do well.

Just be with the most important person in your life; yourself.

Peer pressure and the frantic pace of work created a world where there was no time to listen, no time to be patient, barely time to sleep.

It is only when we are able to step back a while and see things in perspective that we start to get a depth of field. Find a way of sitting with yourself through whatever tradition or technique. Find a space and time to be quiet. It is difficult in the beginning, so make the starting point realistic. Begin with five minutes, and just be with the most important person in your life; yourself.

Effective listening is being empty of thought, being a sponge, focusing your attention and concentration into the energy of the other, it is a genuine opening of ourselves. Practising stillness, it is often surprising how much more aware we become of what is around us. Slowing down our responses and thoughts, assumptions and guesses allows us actually to receive what the other person or nature or music is trying to convey. This is not in the sounds but in the totality of the experience.

Suicide and attempted suicide are a growing problem in our society. Depression and stress, increased pressure and unrealistic expectations have placed many burdens on young shoulders. The group that tries to take their lives most are young men between 16-30, and the age is decreasing. Many of the lives lost had no one close enough to listen to their anguish. In a society that lives in separated age sets, parents are often unaware of the problems encountered by their children or the anxieties they encounter. The time has come, if we are to heal and listen and change, that we turn off our televisions and open the doors. We need to unplug the video games, turn off the noise and listen.

I remember a girl in France who wanted advice about skiing. She talked very quickly and was quite agitated. Her breathing was fast and her body language nervous. She talking about skiing, but soon she was moved on to pressures and worries and her sister being angry all the time. The conversation rambled and there was always the temptation to finish the sentence for her, as one does for someone who never gets to the point. We can all be impatient.

She began to tire herself out, her speech began to slow and finally she paused long enough for me to ask her what was really bothering her. I had read the unspoken language that was calling for help. While not expressed in words this young girl did have some very serious problems and was afraid to share them with friends or family. She was not interested in skiing but really just needed someone to talk to. I made sure that help was found and a solution identified, but I could not have done so if I was only listening to something about skis.

In his book, *The Art of Listening*, Erich Fromm talks about letting go of ourselves and entering the mind of the other person. Much of Fromm's insight encourages listening in new ways and at different levels to what is within. Just as the desert fathers taught emptying the mind, and Zen teaches overcoming desires, many traditions advocate the use of deeper levels of consciousness for spiritual growth. Going beyond the noise of immediate needs and distractions of self preoccupation we can tune into other energies and states of consciousness.

We need to unplug the video games, turn off the noise and listen.

We have all been there, needing to unburden ourselves to someone. It can really hurt if we have to carry things in our hearts alone. Listening comes in many forms, sometimes it needs to be proactive, reaching out to a stranger or a friend, letting them know that we are ready to listen. Other times it is about listening by being present to our own hearts and listening within ourselves. We listen to our bodies when they tell us to rest or eat, and we can tune in to our inner voice when it says, '*enough.*'

The next time someone offers you an opinion, rather than judge or criticize it, see if you can find a grain of truth in what the person is saying. There are so many people we meet, some bright, articulate, interesting but lonely. I have a suspicion that loneliness is intimately linked to our ability to listen.

Listening is a powerful gift and the gateway to sharing another.

Listeners are rarely lonely and rarely dark because they are constantly synergising and connecting, always creating. Listening is power, real power, it awakens in people extraordinary things. Sharon Wilkinson, who has been a close friend for most of my adult life, taught me the art and the gift of listening.

Often when I came to her home I was sucked into a welcome that was all-eclipsing. In her calm delight with the smallest things of my little world I shared my heart and my all. I always emptied my whole being, and she was there, enthralled, awake, wondrous and enthused. She would giggle and delight at my little victories, appease my many vanities and cherish my weaknesses.

Over the decades I have learned a great deal about listening from Sharon.

A young researcher had been a few weeks living with the Maasai nomads for anthropological study. He was briefing me and I was going through the next stages of his research protocol. He had been a little quiet, but I had not been listening to his silence. After I had gone through all the next steps he needed for his study I looked up and he looked down. I asked him what was in his heart and what he felt, and he told me that he was a little home sick and he needed a hug. I sat for over an hour simply giving him a hug, I had been too busy trying to help him and had not properly listened.

A good friend of mine, who is also a colleague, had been going through a difficult time with her husband. Over lunch we talked about relationships, the pain and frustration, she was running the gamut of emotions, and telling Elle and me what she was going through.

I made suggestions and offered a few practical ideas, and I was mid sentence when I saw Elle embracing her as she began to sob, and let it all out. I was thinking, but Elle had been listening, I was reaching for solutions, Elle was reaching for her. Listening is power. None of us is listened to as much as we could be, and each of us can learn to be better listeners.

Listening is a powerful gift and the gateway to sharing another, entering into another, being the other; accepting the other beyond knowing them. It is something that we can all learn to do better.

It is living compassion.

Ask yourself:
Am I quiet when I listen?

Where is my mind when I am listening?

To whom can I listen more carefully to, tomorrow?

A topic for meditation:
Recall something inconsequential that somebody said in the last couple of days, maybe someone you pay little attention to, and allow your meditation to explore what this person said.

Compassion

*Compassion is the expression of the deepest
humanity and the greatest wisdom*

Compassion is not a detached act of selflessness, it is the personal engagement
with the lives of others, coming to them
naturally without effort and leaving
their lives richer and better. Compassion is the power
to be fully human in the touching of each others
fragility and hurt, making whole what was wounded.

Compassion starts deep within us; it is a state of
mind. It is ultimately the energy we pour into life
and the way we see everything. It is life's journey
itself and the light that shines. The world has never
needed compassion as much as it does now.
Compassion is not something we do to help someone
else. If we see it as such, it is a good deed and we
have missed the point. It is not charity or some activ-

ity we are planning for the benefit of others. It is the way in which we see things, so that the goodness within us is expressed as part of our nature. Compassion does not need recognition or affirmation.

Compassion is a way of life, it is the way in which we choose to encounter pain and suffering. It is about bringing our stillness and calm, our experience and humanity into the human condition. It is dynamically relating to the world around us despite ourselves.

I ended my earlier book, *All Will be Well*, with the reflection, 'In the end words matter very little. I have always believed it is our actions, not our thoughts that matter. Tears have never fed a child; pity has never healed a wound. Unless words become deeds, unless dreams are lived they are mere deceptions.

Despite our weakness, because of our frailty we can touch each other with light and change each other with gentleness. We have the power to become light. In a world of brokenness, we can bring wonder. Where there are tears, we can bring laughter. Where there is trembling and loneliness, we can bring love. We were not meant to have compassion, we were meant to become

In the end words matter very little. I have always believed that it is our actions, not our thoughts that matter.

compassionate. With all my heart I believe that this is why we were born.' The greatest healer of all is kindness. Practising the act of compassion changes you in every way. Compassion requires the will to help and the action of giving. It is not an attitude of kindness but a behaviour; it is not words or intentions but what we do. What we do is really who we truly are. We are not what we preach or what we profess; we are not what we hope to be. Compassion is we, ourselves – not the act, but becoming. It is our smile, our attitude, our words, our everything. Helen Keller wrote, 'I long to accomplish a great and noble task, but it is my chief duty to accomplish small tasks as if they were great and noble.'

My friend David Wilkinson, whom I mentioned earlier, is the most unpretentious sorted guy you could meet, he has a self possession and contentment born out of having nothing to prove. David loves the delicious things in life, above all his wife and his sons. He loves jazz, dancing, travelling and scuba diving. Dave has no religion, is not opinionated and has no particular politics or ideology. In many ways you might say that describes people you know too. During the genocides in Uganda, Idi Amin was systematically murdering tribes he believed threatened his dictatorship. Many could not escape in time and as always, the weak and vulnerable were the first to be hacked to death in the bloodbath of Amin's frenzy. Rampaging henchmen searching for outsiders and Amin's enemies wiped out whole communities. David went into the emergency areas, packed his car with children and fled with them over the border into Kenya. He offloaded the children and drove back into Uganda and searched for more he could save and brought them to safety.

As Amin continued his atrocities, David's personal response was to return again and again to find more children to snatch from the clutches of horror and torture. Like all real compassion, there was no flag waving, no publicity, just a quiet personal response to the obvious. The response is entirely our personal energy when faced with darkness and cruelty. It is how we choose to react. It starts with seeing things from within and understanding the world around us as connected.

David's compassion did not start by risking his life for children about to be murdered, nor did it end there. Compassion starts by giving up a seat to someone in a bus, by helping a child after he/she has fallen off his/her bike, by giving someone help before they ask for it. It starts in the minutiae of daily living where we are, here and now. With David, it is reflected in his hospitality, gra-

We were not meant to have compassion, we were meant to become compassionate and in time to become compassion itself.

ciousness and gentleness; his humility is real because he genuinely sees giving humanitarian help as nothing else but obvious. A friend of mine, Amitav Rath, has the philosophy of helping everyone who comes into his life. 'I follow the principle that I have to deal with what is directly in front of me. That is I'm very busy but our measure is how we reach out and touch anyone we can.'

When compassion becomes who we are, it flows into everyone we meet. The hallmarks of the Dr Joes and the Sarunes are the same. The David Wilkinsons and healers who change the world have several things in common. David's Christmas present to his wife was to build a home for a destitute landless group of children in Cambodia; how many husbands would think of such an amazing gift. Each time we move out of our comfort zone, our world becomes more exciting and dynamic.

The first urge is an insatiable appetite to cherish and give, the second is an unconscious flow of happiness that infects those around us and the third is an inspiring sense of delight and wonder as we celebrate everything around us.

> *Until he extends his circle of*
> *compassion to include all living*
> *things, man will not himself find*
> *peace.*

Albert Schweitzer

An old friend once told me, 'Spend a moment, every day, thinking of someone to love.' The last of many letters I got from an old nun in Liverpool was in 1979. Her last line was, 'I always ask myself, "will you remember today forever?" My wish for you is that you give joy Mike, and that you receive it, we will talk on these things soon, God bless.' The Carmelite nun died shortly after at the age of 94.

Compassion seems to be something more than just the things we think, believe or do. The acts that flow from the way of compassion are not counted or seen as good deeds, charity or acts of kindness, they are just natural. There is something about the idea of helping people, giving to charity, being philanthropic and having good intentions that is very different to the idea of compassion.

The dawn of compassion is in our capacity to be kind to our inner self

Compassion is rooted in the vision of sameness and oneness. It is the fusion of what the philosopher Martin Buber identified as the 'I' and the 'Thou,' into 'Us.' Charity often reflects a reference point, where *we* give to *them*. The *them* is not *me*, it is not really the same as myself and so it is not within my inner self. Sensing ourselves as the same fire, the same light and the same energy changes the realisation. The dawn of compassion is in our capacity to be kind to our inner self, and to cherish and respect the child within.

Ask yourself:
Are other people's faiths or beliefs threatening to me?

Have I compassion for myself?

Can I extend compassion to someone who has hurt me?

Do my actions match my values?

Some topics for meditation:
How does happiness fit into my goals?

Do I bring compassion to those around me?

Changing my *reality*

*The way that we choose to see the world
conditions how we will act in it*

To bring gentleness to the child that lives within us we need to touch the power in our hearts. We become unafraid, surprised by the mystery that is right now in our being, not inside our mind but in our being. Every thought is creating our future.

Changing the world is about changing the world we live in. This means changing how we react to it and how we engage it. It means rethinking the way we live, and challenging ourselves constantly.

Neuro-linguistic programming offers us ways to listen to ourselves and our lives, by training, practising, developing the calmness, silence and stillness in the flurry of our daily rush. Greater than every thought, changing our world should be the very focus of our energy.

> *One word or a smile is often*
> *enough to raise up a saddened and*
> *wounded soul.*

Thérèse of Lisieux

What shapes our engagement with the world is the silence that creates us. It is in silence that we find the centre; it is in light that we will find harmony.

To create a new way of looking at everything, takes three things: attitude, thinking and action. We begin by remembering the beautiful people around us and express love and gratitude in the way we live our whole lives, and not merely by single acts. A good beginning is to write down what you really would love to do with your life. The questions we have been considering should be a guide. We need to set our goals, and direct our energies accordingly. We can then look at what we

To create a new way of looking at everything, takes three things: attitude, thinking and action.

need to make happen for the change to occur. The challenge is that we can only live the life that we desire and take power over our own future, when we are prepared to let go of the life we have now. It sometimes seems easier to just complain about the life we have, than to risk leaving the familiar for the unknown.

We are how we live, we become what we do, we are the totality of our actions, we are not what we think, we are not what we believe, but we are in many ways how we treat those around us. We are the humanity we share and the presence we bring. We create ourselves by how we invest our energy. Our character is not manifest in how well we argue or debate nor in our aspirations, but in the tiniest exchanges with each other. Epic acts do not change the world around us, but the myriad of graces we bring into our lives, each smile, each supporting glance, each little act of respect, each gesture of courtesy, each moment we practice patience.

You do not have to have the zeal of Bob Geldof or the passion of Bono to stand up and be counted, you just have to decide to be yourself.

When perception is focused away from the self, frustrations of one's desires have less of a chance to disrupt consciousness. For most people, goals are shaped directly by biological needs and social conventions, and therefore their origins are outside the self. It is amazing how little effort most people make to improve control of attention. To create harmony in whatever one does is the last task that the 'Flow Theory' presents to those who wish to attain 'optimal experience'; it is a task that involves transforming.

It means combining our intelligences to discover wisdom. It means becoming compassion, being the living manifestation of kindness and being dynamically inspirational through how we live, here and now, starting in the only time that matters, the present. Transforming the world around us is an act of conscious, proactive choice. The power is already here and this holistic manner of taking control over our lives gives us incredible freedom.

You do not have to have the zeal of Bob Geldof or the passion of Bono to stand up and be counted, you just have to decide to be yourself, and be passionate about it. We can choose to stay centred in the midst of confusion. We cannot control the universe, but we can control ourselves. Instead of judging ourselves or someone else, we can decide to think positive, energising thoughts. We can give without any expectation in return. Nothing is lost; something is being transformed. We accept love as the healing power in our lives and despite our failures, we keep trying.

Some things that I try to keep in mind are;

Remember the people in your life who inspire you.

Express love and gratitude as often as you can.

Do not navigate your life by the approval of others.

Unlearn all the 'shoulds' and 'oughts' you have been carrying.

Keep and update a chart of all you need to change, all that does not make you happy. Make those changes.

Keep your conversations positive.

Affirm and encourage at every opportunity.

Talk about all the great things happening in your life, all the blessings that surround you.

Grow in science and art, logic and imagination.

Be gracious and courteous.

Be insatiably curious. Learn like a child. Embrace confusion, ambiguity, paradox, and uncertainty.

Laughter

Heart surgeons. psychologists and gurus all agree about one thing – laughter is the best medicine

S preading delight is paramount, there are few things of equal importance. When we see a smiling person and a welcoming open spirit, it is always uplifting. We often forget to laugh or play enough, we need to discover and reclaim joy in our lives. Our cultural conditioning has taught us to be afraid and sceptical, uncertain and untrusting.

In rediscovering authentic pleasure, we will learn deeper levels of humour and simple fun. I am surrounded by people who really celebrate life. Recently I received an honorary degree in Dublin. Dr Caroline Hussey walked at my side in a fabulous procession with Philip Tracey and Martin Sheen. There were seven of us. I asked Caroline what these occasions were for. She gave a wonderful smile and said 'to celebrate. As society becomes richer, there are always less celebrations. There are plenty of dinners and parties but not enough celebration, we need more celebrations.' This is very true. Every day in Africa is a celebration.

The secret is seeing everything with new eyes. This world view is about drawing together many strands of our being in a world that pulls us in many directions. It is about integrating everything in our lives.

I have a friend who loves playing the piano and he practises for hours every week. A young girl I know is a competitive skier, and she lives on the slopes. A man who lives near me wants to learn Swahili, so I hear him all the time playing with the children, learning new words. Changing the way we live and experience the world takes practice. Listen to how we use words, seek opportunities to discover and challenge our own ideas, practise gentleness, develop silence, understand ourselves.

We need to revisit old conclusions, challenge our beliefs and explore ourselves.

We need to question the assumptions of our immediate society and the goals that it sets for us. We need to revisit old conclusions, challenge our beliefs and explore ourselves. We must practise tenderness and self possession. We have to un-clutter our lives from anxieties and worries, to make space for what brings us joy. We need to experience more wonder in the gift of 'now,' and share it with others. We have to awaken grace and mystery in every moment. We need to be the creator of our self-becoming. This means that from now on we shall decide to be awake, decide to be still, decide not to become negative, and decide to share light.

A new us is created by slowly changing the old us, not by annihilation. Most of us only use a fraction of our capacity. By looking differently at how we respond to everything, we can start to channel our powers and gifts into creating a different presence, a different relationship and a different world.

I remember being overwhelmed in the midst of a famine. There were so many starved, hungry children, and we had so little food to give them. To my left there were hundreds of kids standing or sitting, others lying down, behind me there were new arrivals and everywhere else it was worse. A nurse who had been in the tiny mission clinic for many years was pottering around and smiling. I told her it was a little bit too much and that I did not know where to start; how do you begin to change anything when everything is so messed up? She laughed, put her hand on my arm and said, 'Just start with what's in

A new us is created by slowly changing the old us, not by annihilation.

front of you right now and do it with all your heart, then it will be so much easier. Think about this child.' and she handed me a grey, dusty little girl.

I think life is a little bit like that, one smile at a time, one gentle word today, another tomorrow, letting go of worries and learning to trust something greater than ourselves.

Ask yourself:
What makes me laugh?

A topic for meditation:
The energy in laughter.

THE SECRETS OF HAPPINESS

Happiness comes, not from getting what you want, but from nurturing, cherishing and following your passion

Wonder, delight, joy, happiness; these are all about connecting with the flow of energy that joins all of us humans. Our actions create these flows of energy through our prevalent behaviour. In identifying for ourselves what matters and what does not, we can begin to channel our activities and our life force into joyous events. We can learn to let go of surroundings, people and situations that take us away from who we want to be. We should be prepared to leave our job or the place we live if it is not where we ought to be.

A very successful stockbroker who I met was being treated for a heart problem. One of his doctors asked him, what did he really enjoy doing. He thought about it and said, 'More than anything else, I have always wanted to be a musician, singing folk songs and playing my guitar.' It dawned on him that he was killing himself doing what he was trained to do and hated it. He hated the crowded tubes and trains, the rush hour, the ten hour office days and the long business engagements. He realised he would probably end up dying doing something he did not like or want.

He gave up his job, sold his house and moved to Donegal where he sings in pubs, visits friends, and is incredibly happy living his dream.

Why is real joy so elusive, despite all of the things we have? True happiness comes not by getting rid of all our problems, but by

Why is real joy so elusive, despite all of the things we have?

changing our relationship to them. Unrealistic expectations cause us frustration when life doesn't match our preconceived ideas. Celebrating the now becomes inhibited by all the other stuff we cram into our day, stuff which was supposed to help us attain happiness.

Great palaces and cathedrals were not always great, they were built stone by stone, each shaped and hewn, crafted and placed. So too in the cathedral of our lives, it is the countless little changes that create great change, the tiny acts of kindness that create a beautiful life. Despite thousands of years of talking and thinking, we seem nowhere nearer to understanding happiness. People look for power and wealth, popularity and money, but these are only sought because of the incorrect assumption that they will make for a happier life. But what does it mean to be happy? Before we can live happy lives we need to understand for what it is we are searching for. We can decide to be happy by changing the way we view our existence. People who possess inner peace have trained themselves to control their inner experience.

There are many ways to shape the quality of our lives but they all have three things in common:

First, paths to happiness are linked to distinguishing what is essential from what is not.

Second, deeply happy people realise that they create happiness within themselves. It does not come from something external.

Third, happy people rightly assess their self worth,

and they take pleasure from it.

Ronán said, 'One thing to notice about happiness is that it seems much less personal than some other emotions. When you feel depressed, humiliated, afraid, angry, all these things are unmistakably located within you. But happiness seems accidental, as if it didn't belong to you. People often feel distrustful of happiness, as if it might blow away and they wouldn't be able to call it back, while there is no such fear with negative emotions.

'I don't think happiness is an ego emotion. The ego emotions are all to do with possession. Your relationship with your greed or your despair

Happy people rightly assess their self worth, and they take pleasure from it.

is one of possession. Happiness doesn't seem like something you can posses. Indeed, it scares people how easily it seems it could fly away, or be gone in the morning. I think that this is because happiness is 'out there' the way rage is 'in there'. Happiness is something that exists between us and the world - the people, the creatures, the lot, - not inside us. You can open yourself to happiness by opening yourself to the world. But you cannot get it inside you.

'People desperately try to put joy inside them where it will be safe. People tend to abuse the word love, and use it in the sense of "I love hamburgers" or "I love shoes," meaning "I want to consume hamburgers," or "I want to own more and more shoes." This is a forlorn attempt to swallow happiness like a burger or lock it in your wardrobe like a possession. It can never work.

'Opening yourself to the world isn't just opening yourself to the beautiful sunsets over the ocean or the laughter of children or the smell of freshly baked bread. It's also, as you know, the piss and the shit, the violence, the awfulness. But that's the price you pay - entering into a relationship with the world means action, responsibility, like any relationship. And perhaps then you will realise that the best guarantee of the permanence of happiness is exactly because it isn't yours, it's everyone's and no-one's. It's out there for us whether we are there or not.

'Truly happy people have learned to let go of fear, find freedom from the past and celebrate the present. They are capable of understanding the power of the present. Through this freedom they experience profound enjoyment and delight in the now. Their happiness is not some sheltered delusion of a bright decent world, it exists in the reality of now with all our brokenness, and it sheds light on that reality.'

Ask yourself:
What makes me happy?

A topic for meditation:
Your heart's desire.

Gratitude

*Gratitude is healing and empowering, for both the
giver and the recipient*

The smallest acts of kindness generate so
much delight inside us, both when we
give and when we receive that sometimes
we need to stop and look at how we
behave, what we accept as normal. Sometimes we
need to challenge ourselves.

There are many types of gratitude. There is a
mother's unspoken thanks for the gift of her sleeping
child, or the unexpected compliment, the feeling
after a kind word has been spoken to us. Or the
moment we have been surprised by an unexpected
smile.

There is the gratitude we share in friendships, and
the ethereal gratitude of the mystical when creation

touches us, reminding us of a greater mystery. There are the moments when friends express gratitude and the moments we recognise love in our lives. Sometimes we take things for granted, not least the countless gifts we have like sight and hearing. The amazing things that flood our lives every day show the awesome miracles that make up our lives. Each breath, each glance, each sound, every step we take, every new person, everything is a gift; everything is an unexpected opportunity to find delight.

I learned long ago that it is easy to allow my mind to slip into various forms of negativity. It is easy to feel down, easy to feel drained or tired and easier still to become sceptical or sarcastic. When I do fall into these traps, I have noticed that the first thing that leaves me is my sense of gratitude.

All the really happy people I have ever met had in common a childlike sense of gratitude. If you look at the words of Einstein, Ghandi, da Vinci and Newton, they all had a delightful sense of gratitude for the smallest gifts in life.

Einstein, Ghandi, da Vinci and Newton all had a delightful sense of gratitude for the smallest gifts in life.

delightful sense of gratitude for the smallest gifts in life. They shared a powerful exhilaration and enthusiasm together with a realisation that life was a pure gift.

Nothing makes us appreciate how amazing something is until it is taken from us. Often, when we least expect it, something wonderful happens.

Over my years working in Africa, one of the things that amazes me, is the innate sense of thanks that people have. They rejoice all the time, they are delighted and they are grateful for their lives in a very personal and profound way. Often, when we lose this realisation of our gift, we begin to lose so much more as well.

Some topics for meditation:
The Breathing meditation (page 38).

The Forgiveness meditation (page 40).

What am I grateful for today?

Action

Above all, our deeds define us

Our intellect gives us understanding and realisation. With wisdom, we can discern and evaluate, and learn empathy for those around us. But these gifts are worth nothing if they do not lead us into action. Hungry children are not fed on pity, nor do thirsty children drink sympathy. Destitute women can't climb out of poverty with a theory, and anger is no comfort for a girl who has been raped. If our gentleness does not lead to actual, physical reaching out, if our inner calm and stillness do not touch others, they merely stifle as selfishness. Happiness is the key to understanding how we connect to the web of all things. If we are to eliminate suffering, it has to be done "out there." You cannot eliminate suffering inside yourself. Only by opening yourself up to the big "out there," can you go beyond the individual, and be a part of the universal.

We can think and study, read and pray. We can meditate and reflect, understand and become aware. So too, we can become motivated and touched, inspired and enriched. Yet, if all these activities are only for their own sake, then we have learned to fly, only to fold our own wings and leave them unused. Humanity is how we live through our thoughts and words, but above all through our actions,

Humanity is how we live through our thoughts and words, but above all through our actions.

because our deeds define us. The way of action is not theory but reality, it is the living energy we generate around us, how we speak, act, behave towards ourselves and others.

From an early age we have been told what we should and should not do. I remember, like many sons, bringing home my washing for my Mum to do because, 'she likes doing it for me,' just as she liked washing my dishes while I was studying. My mind set would not interpret this behaviour as selfish, in fact I was giving my Mum the opportunity to be Mum.

We rarely see our actions as flawed, we rarely re-examine them and say 'my thinking was wrong on this, my judgement was blind, and my reasoning was way off.' It's only when we deliberately step back, take a look from outside ourselves that we can see something might be worth changing.

The power within comes when we smash down the walls of fear and doubt, when today becomes opportunity and we realise we are unlimited. Perhaps we only see this when we trust our inner voice. The inner light recognises the fire in others, that is when we feel those wordless connections to people.

> *All human actions have one or*
> *more of these seven causes: chance,*
> *nature, compulsion, habit, reason,*
> *passion, and desire.*

Aristotle

It is valuable to remember deeds that have changed us, touched us, helped us be better people. It can be the simplest courtesy, picking up litter from the path, saying hello to someone we pass every day, we can offer our hand to the lonely and reach out to those who are alone. But unless our actions spring from the energy in our hearts they will not be effective. If we look for thanks, recognition, affirmation then we are not behaving according to our nature but acting for approval.

Many old people in Western Europe are ignored and forgotten in a world that is very busy. My childhood friend Tom would often visit old people who were alone, and there were a lot of neglected old people in

Dublin, where Tom and I grew up. Some were very lonely, their only conversation was with shopkeepers or hospital cleaners. Tom visited them, tidied their houses and talked to them. Everything Tom did was in secret. He would secretly slip money through their letter boxes, and would be embarrassed if anyone saw him.

A little girl once came to me and gave me a tiny doll to give to poor children, it was her only doll, she had contracted polio and was blind, but she knew there were other children in the remote African village poorer than she was, who had no little doll. She gave it with a big smile and a heart bigger than herself.

One day on a crowded street in Covent Garden, a teenage girl named Kirsty stopped me. She was shopping for her birthday, and had her heart set on some boots. She looked me in the eye and told me that she remembered a documentary about the children with AIDS for whom our charity cares. She took her birthday envelope from her bag, removed the card from her Mum and Dad and asked me to do something better with the money than buying shiny boots. I took her address and I promised her I would. Her boots translated into treatment for six very ill children who had been abandoned. They would otherwise be dead today, and instead the are at

The power within comes when we smash down the walls of fear and doubt.

school. Action is eloquence.

Few people see inside us, or look behind our protective masks. I had given a dozen talks in a week, trying to find aid for a famine that no one really took seriously. At a lunch party, I saw a lot of real friends. It was a welcoming home, full of great people, the successful and the beautiful. I was returning to Africa with enough support to feed 12,000 children but I knew that there were 160,000 who were starving. I prepared to leave the party early and head for the airport, and I suddenly felt lost and alone.

It does not take great things, just little things with great love to change everything.

I knew what I was returning to, and felt my heart torn out of me. A feeling of utter failure flushed through me, with a sense of desolation and fear. There was anguish in me and in that moment, the frightening sense that I did not belong any more in my own country. I wanted to go because I felt weak and vulnerable, empty and fragile. As I left, Gillian came to the doorstep to say goodbye. All she did was put both her arms around me. Gillian is tiny and I had to bend down to embraced her. She did not say anything, she just hugged me for a long time. God, I needed that hug. I was feeling so, so alone and part of me was just no longer able to bear seeing suffering and pain all the time. I was afraid. I felt I always had to be everyone else's strength, but in that moment it was I who needed a hug. Gillian knew loss and grief and she whispered to me 'I know,' and I knew that she did. I cried my eyes out many times that day but it was that simple hug that gave me the leg up when I really needed it.

You met Morten Skovdal before when we spoke about change. He was the young Danish student who came to work with me. Before then he was based in London and wanted to make a difference in the world. Blonde, blue eyed and intelligent he could do anything he wanted, his friends were successful and wealthy. Morten was trendy, funky, funny and like any up-and-coming professional. Morten goes clubbing, partying, works hard and plays harder. In the two years I have known him he has raised $500,000 for AIDS prevention, orphans, women's groups and diarrhoea projects. He is self effacing, really cool and very Danish. But in everything he does, it is about action, the doing, not the talk.

> *You cannot have a proud and chivalrous spirit if your conduct is mean and paltry; for whatever a man's actions are, such must be his spirit.*

Demosthenes

You also met Billy before when we spoke about dreams. He saw the poverty, the diseases and the challenges we faced. He also visited a terminal care programme in which we were caring for thousands of AIDS victims. His wife Lynn was an accountant who retrained as a nurse for the terminally ill. The next I heard from Billy was a year later when a container with a million dollars worth of medical equipment and medicines arrived. ICROSS in Canada now sends over $2 million a year to poor countries.

Terenure College in Dublin is a well known school in Ireland. My classmates and I set up the International Community for Relief of Starvation and Suffering, ICROSS. The idea was born while we were still at school. For nearly 30 years most of our support came from the extended network we developed, and past pupils and friends all pitched in. We raised over $16 million in a decade and now a new generation of teenagers are involved. Fasts, campaigns, fancy dress days, plays, dances, anything they can think of. It does not take great things, just little things with great love to change everything. If we can get schools sowing the seeds of action, we can spark fires in young hearts that will set the whole world on fire.

We can reach out to change our wounded world in many ways. One way is to fight ignorance and hatred. Crimes of hatred are on the rise and examples of senseless persecution are all too common. Each of us can fight against bigotry starting with the conversations we have with friends. Mean jokes about Islam, cruel words about ethnicity, demeaning remarks about women; all these are offered in the name of humour, a bit of fun. In reality words can have a deeply corrosive effect, not only in the dialogue itself, but also in the atmosphere around us. Rabbi Daniela Thau, who worked tirelessly to edit this book, has spent her life fighting hatred. Whether it is prejudice between Muslims and Jews or Jews and Christians, whether it is in the Middle East, suburban England, Germany or India, she works to bring understanding and dialogue by talking with those in conflict and challenging the sources of hatred and intolerance. In a time when our society harbours so much prejudice and loathing against people who are 'different,' we all have critical roles to play in extinguishing the fires of fear and distrust that are smoulder against minority communities.

> *You do not have to believe in a God to change the world*

You do not have to believe in a God to change the world, and many of my close friends who rejected the hypocrisy of religion have been the incarnations of selfless compassion. The challenge before the human race is to champion love and equality. We may all have examples in our lives of people who have really awoken us, people whose actions have lived the philosophies about which others only write. Talk is cheap. Sharon Wilkinson, of whom I have written before, is a woman I met while she was working in the slums of Africa improving women's health. Sharon was a nurse who believed in people's right to determine their own future. In the twenty years I have known her she has always celebrated everything, everyone and delighted in the adventure. If action means anything, it is about giving ourselves, it is about fidelity and sharing ourselves. Sharon adopted and fostered children, educated strangers, created opportunities where none existed. Often, her deeds are invisible and anonymous, because she does not work to a public agenda. She simply remedies things that are amiss. Sharon only ever gave from inside herself, her whole self, and only with delight. There are those who have little and give it all and those who give a little from vast wealth. Sharon gives it all. She gives with her everything, mindless of the measure or the worth of the receiver and without judgement.

> *Through the hands of such as these*
> *God speaks,*
> *and from behind their eyes,*
> *He smiles upon the earth.*

Khalil Gibran

If we look at the examples of humanity that has enriched us, we will find the same threads of power over and over again; the Dalai Lama, Helen Keller, Nelson Mandela. These people may be quite ordinary but they are other-centred. There is no point in personal enlightenment other than for our own personal elation. Spiritual intelligence is worth having only for the love that it generates. This is the secret of change, to generate and to give away love in the smallest fabric of our lives.

A mystic called John of the Cross said that this giving of love is not all about acts of kindness or giving, it is not about trying to do something, it is about being love itself, 'We stop trying to make particular acts through our thinking, we become more a part of the total, one wholeness, a pure energy, a calm interior stillness that generates it, you don't have to understand or explain it, the less we understand, the more we penetrate into the night of the spirit.'

The freedom to delight in ourselves, and to rejoice in the wonder of life's opportunities is a gift.

The freedom to delight in ourselves, and to rejoice in the wonder of life's opportunities is a gift. It can at once revolutionise all of our thinking and transform our world into an exciting discovery of new things, where everything is gift and the countless wonders are seen through different eyes. This is not about euphoric enthusiasm but a gradual restructuring of the way we see everything and everyone starting with our inner being. It is an awakening at a very intimate level, it is the most exhilarating and amazing, empowering and liberating experience.

If you and I are going to change the face of extreme poverty, we must all of us become actively involved. Find a group near you, don't only send money but become active. Whether the Red Cross or Comic Relief, Action Aid or GOAL, there are many great groups fighting hard against the obscenities and horrific suffering destroying our world. If you only do one thing from reading this book, get involved in something global, there are hundreds of excellent passionate groups of people who need you.

If your interest is the torture of the innocent, there are movements like Amnesty International that I belong to, struggling against oppression. If you want to help the children of the world there is Save the Children, World Vision, CARE, Concern, Water Aid. There are many very small organisations like my own ICROSS and Kids for Kids and Child to Child, all working together for a better world. There is plenty to choose from. Whatever you do, start now to help fight suffering anywhere, everywhere.

> **Ask yourself:**
> *What will take me closer to my goals tomorrow?*
>
> *What will it take to turn my dreams into actions?*
>
> **A topic for meditation:**
> *A cherished dream.*

And Saralunar spoke softly to the young man who was looking across the valley below, drinking deeply the words that were spoken to him. His head was bowed and his eyes closed, his hair covered his face. 'Live by the fires within you, walk by your own path, create your own today and live with the wind. Taste always the new and dance to the music within your dream, sing that song. Do not listen to the voices of the many or walk with the crowd or dance the same dance as them. Follow the voice that has awakened you, but listen carefully to it as it will only speak to you in your dreams. Trust what makes you smile. Seek stillness, if you have noise in your head you will be noisy, if your mind is calm you will bring calm. Be joy in your moments and it will follow you into each hour, let your way of life be yours. Know the child that lives in you and befriend the mystic within your heart. If you are to have a true path to your days, let go of all, save love and kindness, for these are lights that will become you.'

And what about changing the world?

☯☯☯☯

Give light, and the darkness will disappear of itself.

Erasmus

When we are balanced and strong, in our body and our intelligences, and when we act with clear intent, we affect all that is around us. We cannot think our way to an integrated life, we have to live it. We cannot learn joy, we have to release it from inside us. The spiritual synergy is already in us, it just needs to be awoken. Whatever our beliefs, backgrounds or life models, drawing our energies together into one force will transform our world. If we channel our intellect, creativity, wonder, sensuality and vision, our thinking is driven by all of the energies that give us delight and happiness.

Change occurs when our inner being transforms and we see ourselves as light. Not as a physical being wading through the experiences of life on a material plane, but as beings of spiritual power, acting through a physical body .

We need to act in a kind and peaceful way. If our lives are to stand for peace and kindness, we must do kind and peaceful things. The greatest wealth in our life comes from our ability to love ourselves. We are so much more than we can think ourselves to be, we are pure power, pure energy, already immortal.

> *If our lives are to stand for peace and kindness, we must do kind and peaceful things.*

We possess the gift of life and with each day a new opportunity comes with the potential to be whatever we choose. We learn to value others, and to treat ourselves well, by learning and maintaining a high degree of self-worth.

> *Care for yourself, respect yourself, make sure you are cherished and nurtured.*
>
> *Wherever you go, celebrate it.*
>
> *Feed your body, look after it and feed your mind. Avoid junk food for both.*
>
> *Respect yourself actively, in thought, word and deed.*
>
> *Listen to your heart, inform your emotions, unlearn negative habits and create space for*

> *yourself to grow and love.*
>
> *Build on your strengths and gently overcome your weaknesses.*
>
> *Laugh every day.*
>
> *Forgive your failures and listen to your inner voice.*
>
> *Be still and find calmness.*
>
> *Make time to celebrate and enjoy your own company. Be a true friend to your self.*
>
> *Tune in to the languages of your body and your heart. Listen to what they tell you.*

Happiness is innate within us, and how we connect with it is a choice. Thinking doesn't take us to happiness; acceptance, inspiration and action do. Once we let go of the fears and habits that trap us into lifestyles that do not serve us well, we can experience levels of wonder that will transform everything we are.

As well as transforming ourselves dynamically, we can change everyone around us through our own energy and attitude. We have all come across people who inject inspiration and life into everything; they express delight into their environment naturally. This creative change occurs when we are around people, though verbal communication may not always be necessary. It is good to remember that all we have shall some day be given away, and the only thing we take from this earth is what we gave away.

Everything we do should create the energy and power of love, and celebrate ourselves and each other. Not just with parties and dinners but to celebrate each other's miracle and gift. We ought to do this every day, and be as kind as we can be. With kindness and compassion,

Everything we do should create the energy and power of love, and celebrate ourselves and each other.

we can see that other people's worries, their pain and their frustrations, are every bit as real as our own - and often far worse. By recognising this and trying to offer some assistance, we open our hearts and enhance our own sense of gratitude. There is always a parallel between our attitude towards strangers and our overall level of happiness. The life-force in us draws its energy from the direction and content we give our lives.

Lin Yutang said, 'I have done my best.' That is about all the philosophy of living that one needs. Francis Maitland Balfour said, 'The best thing to give to your enemy is forgiveness; to an opponent, tolerance; to a friend, your heart; to your child, a good example; to a father, deference; to your mother, conduct that will make her proud of you; to yourself, respect;

to all men, charity.' Giving is the realisation that the stranger is part of you, and that you share his or her need.

Write down questions that are meaningful to you where you are, here and now. These may be very personal or general, do not concern yourself with the nature of the questions, what matters is that you challenge yourself.

They might be questions like:
Am I gentle with myself?

Am I open to intimacy?

Am I too attached to the past?

Is dissatisfaction an incentive or an excuse?

What could I do tomorrow to be more in charge of my destiny?

How does happiness fit into my goals?

We are all very different, and our uniqueness is what makes us all worthy of respect, from each and all of us. The love that we feel for others, and the appreciation we have for our own special qualities, increases as we respect one another and ourselves more. We should live everyday like New Year's Day. We can foster the habit of making people feel good, affirming and complimenting them. Many people go through their entire lifetimes wishing that other people would acknowledge them. We all may know some of those people.

> *Just as love is an orientation which*
> *refers to all objects and is*
> *incompatible with the restriction to*
> *one object, so is reason a human*
> *faculty which must embrace the*
> *whole of the world with which man*
> *is confronted.*

Erich Fromm

The difference between being happy and being unhappy is not how often we get low, or even how low we drop, but how we cope with our low moods. How do we relate to our changing feelings? Positive and negative feelings both come and go. Radical change happens not through massive shifts, it starts with tiny things, that grow into patterns.

Radical change happens not through massive shifts, but with tiny things that grow into patterns.

It grows into approaches and habits, slowly becoming part of the framework of our days. It etches itself onto our face, and is reflected in our words and our life style. In everything we do, we become more that energy and force through which we choose to live our days. It is our 'us.' It is the very deepest imagining and the most immediate reaction, it is in our walking, listening, touching and relating. Changing our now is about becoming living compassion through listening, through seeing wonder, tasting mystery and breathing gentleness into our world. It is becoming the happiness we want to see in the world, despite the storms and tides.

IRENEUS – A JOURNEY *part IV* ═══════════════════

Saralunar held Ireneus by the hand as he awakened Ireneus' inner voice to the sacred buried within. He spoke but not in words, and his silence shared truths that have no knowing, only living. 'My child, receive each day as a new gift that is a miracle and everything in it as a wonder. See with the eyes of a newborn infant. Let go of anxieties in your head, passing them into your breath so their ghosts do not haunt you. Love is the truth that lies at the heart of creation and is the substance of our souls, but love of all creation, not only those who hold us in their arms.' Ireneus was born into a different world with beauty all about and light within, a fire grew in him as Saralunar spoke to his soul. 'There is mystery in all things, transforming the trees and stars, animals and birds, rain and sky. The invisible speaks to you in each breath and in each moment given to you in creation. It has no words and is only uttered in silence for everlasting. Everything lies in this love. This is our reason, to find the One that dwells within, and open the gates to discover the light inside you. Be quiet enough to know what to say with your actions. Never limit yourself, live the impossible, always step beyond yourself. Death is not putting out the light, it is only blowing out the candle as dawn has come. This is what you were born to be, to become light.'

Long did Ireneus taste these words and smell the fragrance of the incense, and when he raised his head, Saralunar had left, passing into the clouds, but as Ireneus began the journey home, he was not alone and within him dwelt mystery.

In the end, changing the world is really this. To celebrate all that we have, to share stillness, to give from the oceans of our heart, to create joy from the fire in our hearts, and to cherish life for the miracle that it is.

ACKNOWLEDGEMENTS

Where we are, who we are and the light within us is a living tapestry of our experience. The fabric of our lives is in part the surprises, the fears and battles, the bruises and hurts. It is also the wonder and laughter, celebration and delight. Life throws at us countless things that can often knock us down and it is our friends who pick us up. In sharing these reflections about what we can do in this world I have shared only the adventure of my own journey. The friends who have walked with me have filled my life with grace and laughter, and have never ceased to amaze me. Many of those I thank are in the pages of Changing the World as I have shared their stories which have enriched my own life. Throughout this book Ronán Conroy has brought his rare insights and gentleness. Colin Meagle, who delights in the gift of life, encouraged me, and Joe Barnes walked silently at my side enjoying the discovery. Stephen Sackur challenged me with real and honest questions. There are many who have honoured me with their inner selves, sharing their deepest struggles and wounds, and I hold them in my heart. There are those who hold my hand and sing with me and those who always welcome me into their home. They are the people who accept me as I am and they celebrate me just as I am. We can all find the gifts through which we can change ourselves, each other, the whole world - one step at a time.

Michael Meegan

Rift Valley, Kenya

eyeBookshelf

THE AMERICAS / ASIA

	Thunder & Sunshine *Alastair Humphreys*	The Good Life *Dorian Amos*	The Good Life *Dorian Amos*	The Good Life Gets Better *Dorian Amos*	Cry From the Highest Mountain *Tess Burrows*	Riding the Outlaw Trail *Simon Casson & Richard Adamson*	Trail of Visions Route 2 *Vicki Couchman*	Riding with Ghosts *Gwen Maka*	Riding with Ghosts – South of the Border *Gwen Maka*	Lost Lands Forgotten Stories *Alexandra Pratt*	Frigid Women *Sue & Victoria Riches*	Touching Tibet *Niema Ash*	First Contact *Mark Anstice*	Tea for Two *Polly Benge*	Baghdad Business School *Heyrick Bond Gunning*
eyeThinker		•	•	•			•		•	•	•		•	•	•
eyeAdventurer	•	•	•		•		•	•	•	•	•		•	•	•
eyeQuirky							•								•
eyeCyclist	•							•	•					•	
eyeRambler															
eyeGift	•														
eyeSpiritual															

THE AMERICAS   **ASIA**

AFRICA / EUROPE

	Moods of Future Joys *Alastair Humphreys*	Green Oranges on Lion Mountain *Emily Joy*	Zohra's Ladder *Pamela Windo*	Walking Away *Charlotte Metcalf*	Changing the World from the inside out *Michael Meegan*	All Will Be Well *Michael Meegan*	Seeking Sanctuary *Hilda Reilly*	Crap Cycle Lanes *Captain Crunchynutz*	50 Quirky Bike Rides...in England and Wales *Rob Ainsley*	On the Wall with Hadrian *Bob Bibby*	Special Offa *Bob Bibby*	The European Job *Jonathan Booth*	Fateful Beauty *Natalie Hodgson*	Slow Winter *Alex Hickman*
eyeThinker		•	•	•	•	•	•		•			•	•	•
eyeAdventurer	•	•						•			•	•	•	
eyeQuirky							•	•	•		•	•		
eyeCyclist	•						•	•	•					
eyeRambler									•	•	•			
eyeGift	•						•	•						
eyeSpiritual				•	•									

AFRICA   **EUROPE**

eyeBookshelf

ASIA / AUS

	Jungle Janes — Peter Burden	Trail of Visions — Vicki Couchman	Desert Governess — Phyllis Ellis	Fever Tress of Borneo — Mark Eveleigh	My Journey with a Remarkable Tree — Ken Finn	The Jungle Beat — Roy Follows	Siberian Dreams — Andy Home	Behind the Veil — Lydia Laube	Good Morning Afghanistan — Waseem Mahmood	Jasmine and Arnica — Nicola Naylor	Prickly Pears of Palestine — Hilda Reilly	Last of the Nomads — W J Peasley	Travels in Outback Australia — Andrew Stevenson
eyeThinker		•	•		•	•	•		•		•	■	•
eyeAdventurer	•		•		•	•	•	•	•			■	
eyeQuirky			•	•								■	
eyeCyclist												■	
eyeRambler												■	
eyeGift		•										■	
eyeSpiritual													

EUROPE / CROSS CONTINENT

	The Accidental Optimist's Guide to Life — Emily Joy	Con Artist Handbook — Joel Levy	Forensics Handbook — Pete Moore	Travels with my Daughter — Niema Ash	Around the World with 1000 Birds — Russell Boyman	Death — Herbie Brennan	Discovery Road — Tim Garratt & Andy Brown	Great Sects — Adam Hume Kelly	Blood Sweat and Charity — Nick Stanhope	Triumph Around the World — Robbie Marshall	Traveller's Tales from Heaven and Hell — Various	Further Traveller's Tales from Heaven and Hell — Various	More Traveller's Tales from Heaven and Hell — Various
eyeThinker	■	•	•	•		•	•	•					
eyeAdventurer			•		•	•		•		•			
eyeQuirky	■		•		•		•			•	•	•	•
eyeCyclist						•	•						
eyeRambler													
eyeGift	■	■				•		•			•	•	•
eyeSpiritual						•		•					

eye**Bookshelf**

All Will be Well
£9.99

In a time when the world is in so much turmoil and con-fusion, self – help books are on the increase. This is a book, however, which does not focus on the self. Instead it looks at how love and compassion when given out to others, whether through a simple smile or by holding a dying soul, can act as a better antidote to the often painful human condi-tion.

Blood Sweat & Charity
£9.99

The only charity challenge guidebook to help you through any or all of the process; from identifying the challenge or the cause, to how to document it and maximise the fundraising and awareness along with making sure that you are physically prepared for whatever you take on.

www.eye-books.com

eye**Bookshelf**

Moods of Future Joys
£7.99

Alastair Humphreys' round the world journey of 46,000 miles was an old-fashioned adventure: long, lonely, low-budget and spontaneous. Moods of Future Joys recounts an epic journey that succeeded through Humphreys' trust in the kindness of strangers, at a time where the interactions of our global community are more confused and troubled than ever.

Cry from the Highest Mountain
£9.99

If you wanted to express a really important message that would affect the future of humanity – you could do worse than shout it from the highest mountain. The mission was to promote Earth Peace by highlighting Tibet and the Dalai Lama's ideals as an arrow of light for the new millennium. For Tess it became a struggle of body and mind, as she was compelled towards the highest point within herself.

www.eye-books.com